P9-DUY-504

SURFERS OF THE
ZUVUYA

SURFERS OF THE ZUVUYA

TALES OF INTERDIMENSIONAL TRAVEL

by José Argüelles

Introduced by
Marilyn Ferguson

BEAR & COMPANY
SANTA FE, NEW MEXICO

Library of Congress Cataloging-in-Publication Data

Argüelles, José, 1939-
    Surfers of the Zuvuya: tales of interdimensional travel / by José
Argüelles.
      p.   cm.
    Bibliography: p.
    ISBN 0-939680-55-6: $9.95
    1. Voyages to the other world. 2. Astral projection.
3. Argüelles, José, 1939-   . I. Title.
BF1999.A6397 1988
133.9 — dc19   88-18091
                                                                       CIP

Bear & Company
Santa Fe, NM 87504-2860

Cover photo collage: José Argüelles
Cover photo: Russ McDougal
Text illustrations: José Argüelles
Cover & interior design: Kathleen Katz
Frontispiece calligraphy: Loring Palmer
Typography: Buffalo Publications, Santa Fe

Printed in the United States of America by R.R. Donnelley

9 8 7 6 5 4 3 2 1

FOR JOSH_____*In death*
as in life
we are one

TABLE OF
CONTENTS

FOREWORD

When I first met José Argüelles at the front door of my house in Los Angeles on a bright December day in 1983, we exchanged the kind of warm greetings typical of writers favorably acquainted with each other's work. I admired his elegant and literary *Transformative Vision* and had quoted it in a book I wrote, *The Aquarian Conspiracy*. I also knew of him as coauthor of a beautiful art volume, *Mandala*.

Within a few minutes he had unfurled the inspired series of paintings that later became the center of his book, *Earth Ascending*. José had come to lunch, and my husband and I were so entertained and enlightened that he stayed for two days. That set the pattern for future meetings, which tended to happen in places like the Brussels Hilton or the teepees of the Ojai Foundation (California). Nothing about José is less than mythic.

His early environment was, as he put it, "calculated to keep me on edge." His father was a Mexican with strong Communist leanings; his mother, a romantically inclined German-American Lutheran. He was reared biculturally and bilingually, living his first few years in Mexico, then moving to Minnesota. "My twin brother Ivan was my salvation," he said. "He was equally odd, but at least we had each other."

José worked at a multitude of jobs: filing books at a public library, rising at four a.m. to deliver papers, washing windows, washing dishes, unloading hundred-pound salt bags from freight trains.

Since he was a visual artist, an advanced degree in art history seemed appropriate. He spent time in Europe as a

graduate scholar, "a Renaissance kid." He painted murals at
colleges in the late 1960s and early 1970s; later he became
an art critic in Boulder, Colorado. In 1970, while teaching at
the University of California at Davis, he organized the first
Whole Earth Festival. "One reason that I got a Ph.D.," José
once told me, "was that I'd known for some time that I had
to acquire a cloak of legitimacy if I didn't want to be treated
as a lunatic. I'd had my first vision when I was around four,
so I knew from an early age that there was something different
about me."

He also became a student of Tibetan Buddhism. "Even
with a Ph.D., it's hard to get away with being a visionary. I
found I had to develop a lot of compassion and spirituality.
Otherwise I could have become embittered — a nasty Bohemian
sitting in a coffeehouse sniping at society. I trained myself to
accept being attacked."

From the early days of our friendship I remember José
talking about August 16 and August 17, 1987, dates he considered auspicious for a "Harmonic Convergence" celebration.
He had several reasons: personal inspiration, his interpretation
of the Mayan mind, and the modern prophecy of several North
American tribes. As the reader of *Surfers of the Zuvuya* will
discover, José Argüelles takes revelation and prophecy both
lightly and seriously.

Grassroots response to the idea of the convergence was
strong and growing stronger by mid-1987, when the media
discovered it. It was soon billed as a New Age, flaky, apoc-
alyptic extravaganza; despite the media interpretation, the
event attracted millions of sane celebrants who were glad of
a chance to pray or meditate for peace and for the welfare
of the embattled planet.

One thing became evident: *Our culture has little under-
standing of the purpose of myth or the role of mythmaker.*
Myths are not for believing or disbelieving. They are for using.
If a myth or a metaphor works in revamping our deepest

values, it is truer than the evening news or the textbook
fact. Myth, poetry, art, and music are truths of a different
dimension — sustenance and regeneration for the tired spirit.
The human brain learns best by story, by game, by a framework
of meaning.

The Mayan myth, as interpreted by José Argüelles in *The
Mayan Factor, Earth Ascending,* and *Surfers of the Zuvuya,*
is a "circle whose center is everywhere and whose circumference
is nowhere." It is elaborated by the force of imagination. It
resonates with our finer possibilities ... the power of the
"inert" placebo to relieve pain, the power of intention to alter
the subtlest of physiological events, the power of expectation
to influence what we see and hear.

Our stories should resonate with our finer possibilities.
The Harmonic Convergence was such a story from a modern
mythmaker, enacted on a scale that would have impressed
the ancients. *Surfers of the Zuvuya* is a helpful and inspiring
next-step story for the patriots of Earth.

On October 29, 1987, after the Harmonic Convergence,
José's bright and beloved eighteen-year-old son Josh was killed
in an automobile accident.

José dealt with this great loss with his customary complete-
ness. He went into a prolonged period of isolation (called the
49-day Bardo Retreat in the Tibetan tradition) and emerged
having consolidated his love and grief into a new creation.
This book is a gift to and from José, a light that emerged
from his darkest hour.

Each of the half-dozen or so times I have spent with José
has been magical. Just as "Thirteen" is the middle name of
Uncle Joe Zuvuya in this story, "Magic" is the middle name
of Uncle José. Welcome to a philosophical adventure with a
man who lives his dream and dreams his life. Surf's up!

MARILYN FERGUSON
Los Angeles, California
June 14, 1988

PREFACE

This tale of my encounter with my dimensional double, Uncle Joe Zuvuya, is intimately connected with a saga of life and death. Scarcely a month after I had first written this whimsical little text, at 2:35 AM, October 29, 1987, my eighteen-year-old son, Josh, along with his buddy, Mike Buddington, were instantly killed in a head-on automobile collision outside of Fort Collins, Colorado.

Informed of this news by a police officer at 7:00 AM, October 29, my world also came instantly to a halt. As I have slowly come to deal with this reality, which has been the most crucial, destiny-altering event in my life, I have inevitably come to wonder about the relationship between my dimensional double and the events leading up to and following Josh's death. It has occurred to me more than once that my son's voice — or that of his dimensional double — came to inform my dimensional double, prompting me to write this book. Why?

Death is the most direct and irrevocable entrance we have to the next dimension. Up until the writing of this text, I had not fully focussed my attention and energy on interdimensional reality. True, I was aware of it and had had more than my share of experiences that penetrated the veil. But nothing in my experience had yet dictated to me the need for a continued, enduring relationship with interdimensional reality.

When I began to write *Surfers of the Zuvuya* in mid-September, 1987, Josh had barely begun his freshman year of college at Colorado State University in Fort Collins. Nonetheless, our relationship had entered a new phase and our communication, both by telephone and letter, was definitely up-leveled. Our sense of common identity was affirmed and strengthened through these communications. Indeed, part of my inspiration for writing *Surfers* had to do with my need to communicate, in a more simple language, the meaning and import of Harmonic Convergence for people such as my son and his generation.

On Sunday night, October 25, Josh called me. He had misplaced his car key and asked me to send him my key to the '78 Honda he had inherited from my wife and me for his high school graduation present. There was something in his voice that was uncharacteristic, as if he were ever so slightly desperate. The next morning I wrapped the key in a piece of cardboard and enclosed a note. The last words in my note to him were "Harmonic Convergence is still happening — look out for the UFOs!" This was our last communication.

My son was out with his buddy at 2:35 AM because earlier that evening Mike had left his keys in the nearby town of Greeley. Josh was driving Mike back from Fort Collins to Greeley for a second time that night in order to retrieve Mike's keys. But the key that turned the ignition for that post-midnight ride became the key to the kingdom. Without warning, the reality of the next dimension intervened.

The matter of the keys stuck with me. For one thing, I knew that Josh's death was the key for me into what I call the Great Mystery, the interdimensional reality that totally penetrates and informs *this* physical reality, which we too often assume to be the "only reality." In the weeks and months following Josh's death, I began to realize that *Surfers of the Zuvuya* had been prophetic, for now my whole being is immersed in an exploration of interdimensional reality. Let me explain how this has come about.

Surfers of the Zuvuya arose spontaneously as an answer to immediate post-Harmonic Convergence needs — my own and yours. My previous book, *The Mayan Factor: Path Beyond*

Technology, which was so closely associated with the Convergence, is a challenging philosophical and technical book. It
deserves to be studied, and hopefully it will be studied for a
long time after Harmonic Convergence. However, given the
unanticipated popular response to Harmonic Convergence,
August 16-17, 1987, I knew that there was a need to create
an equally popular way of telling people about the Convergence.

Precisely because so many people responded to the powerful
energy of those days without knowing the reason behind the
Convergence, *Surfers of the Zuvuya* sprang into being. It was
like a deep undercurrent that swept up from within me, with
tidal ripples that extended to the far reaches of the Earth. That
the theme of this book was interdimensional reality delighted
me and took even me by surprise, yet it was a natural follow-
up to my own personal journey after the Convergence.

For the moment, let's just say that Harmonic Convergence
is a real life, real time chapter in a multidimensional Mayan
saga. It is a saga of which the mute stones of Mayan ruins
are but the merest hint, for the vastness of this epic saga still
lies enscribed in *the future*.

During the time of the Convergence, everybody from
Shirley MacLaine and Johnny Carson to nameless thousands
in small towns across the USA and the world — from Leningrad
in the USSR to sunny Rio de Janeiro — got swept up into the
act. And yet, most of those people scarcely knew why. They
felt *something* and knew that it was time to do ... this thing.
Get up at some unlikely hour and salute the sun? Why?

Because all of us, as outrageous as it may sound, had
been zapped by the *Zuvuya!* Yes. What people *felt* was the
call and the tickle of the *Zu-vu-ya*.

Zuvuya is the Mayan term for the big memory circuit. It
is the memory hotline. It works individually and collectively.
Most importantly, *it connects equally to the future as well as
to the past*. Why? Because the Zuvuya is the *interdimensional
thread*. And we are all interdimensional.

You can enter the Zuvuya any time, and any place. Once
you enter it, you realize you have never been out of touch
with it. But when you are out of touch with it, well, nothing
makes any sense. And yet the Zuvuya is always there. It is
what fuels synchronicity, and consequently, it is the pipeline
for magic.

In the styrofoam wasteland of our technological supermarket lives, Harmonic Convergence happened, and it was
and is our entrance into the larger magical, mythical, mystical
life of the galaxy. Harmonic Convergence was and is the
interdimensional zap of the Zuvuya riding the consciousness
of the human race, giving it *the signal* that something else is
going on. What is going on is the fact that we are not alone.
Yes, there is life beyond and within planet Earth — and lots
of it.

By listening to this signal and tracking it to its source,
everything changed for me. I became a *surfer of the Zuvuya*
by learning how to play interdimensionally. When you learn
to ride the Zuvuya, you can double your pleasure in life. It
is *not* that far out.

We are all familiar with the magic carpet ride that appeared
in the movies of the 1940s and 1950s. Of course, that image
came to us from Arabian fairy tales. But what is the magic
carpet ride? It is a metaphor for interdimensional travel.

In the same way, through the rise of surfing in the sixties
and seventies, we received another image: that of riding the
crest of a wave from one dimension of reality to the next.
The Zuvuya is the wave, and to surf this wave is to be at the
dynamic crest that interfaces our third-dimensional physical
reality with the reality of the fourth-dimension — the dimension
of our dream bodies, energy bodies, or light bodies. Collectively then, Harmonic Convergence was the cresting of a
solar-galactic Zuvuya wave that naturally brought our planet
bubbling in its wake.

Through becoming a surfer of the Zuvuya, I began to see

how much Harmonic Convergence had affected me. It would be trite to say that it changed my life. That would sound like I was trying to sell you something or make a confessional on behalf of a television salvation soap opera. It is more accurate to say that Harmonic Convergence became my life. But that is only because my life had become Harmonically Converged.

For years I had followed my own voice, the voice inside my head. That is how I got to those mysterious dates, August 16 and 17, 1987. It was not just the voice inside my head that I followed. It was also my lifetime pursuit of the equally mysterious Maya.

Then Harmonic Convergence occurred. The voice inside my head got empowered. It took over. And when it took over I realized that I myself had become a character in a vast and awesome, multidimensional Mayan epic, a giant tale within a tale, a galactic story of cosmic proportions!

The voice inside my head turned out to be Uncle Joe Zuvuya, my "dimensional double." You see, the real meaning of Harmonic Convergence, for me, was the arrival of — and conscious joining of forces with — my dimensional double. I suspect this may be the case with many of us who tapped into our "converged" selves.

Needless to say, I have been aware of my Uncle Joe for a long time. But it took Harmonic Convergence to spring Uncle Joe into action. In fact, I was surprised when he showed up. But once he did show up, I saw the wisdom of his timing. After all, Uncle Joe Zuvuya is a Mayan, and the Maya are the ringmasters in the grand circus of time.

Because of the Mayan facility with time, questions of prophecy, precognition and body doubles are but tricks in the Mayan's deck of interdimensional cards. In this deck, past and future are easily shuffled through the present. Precisely for this reason, I have developed an almost haunted feeling about the relationship between the emergence of my dimensional double and the death of my son — and his consequent return into the Great Mystery. Did my dimensional double show up for me as a gift or a sign to break me into the reality of the "other side?" As I was going through my own post-Convergence sorting out of things, was my son's dimensional double benignly plugged into me, prompting Uncle Joe to break into full character?

There is no question that some mysterious connection exists between the writing of this book and my son's death. The widening web of interdimensional reality encompasses facets of reality that are closed to the doors of logic and reason. Confronted with such synchronistic or cosmically introduced enormities — accidents we call them — all that can be done is to take a leap. And leaping — or should I say surfing? — just ahead of myself is Uncle Joe, forever teaching me to lighten up and ride the swirling tidal currents of the imagination.

As a result of his insistence that I experiment and grow, this book is a decidedly different book than its predecessor, *The Mayan Factor*, in just about every way you can imagine except one. Both books take as their point of departure that mysterious cosmic ingredient, the Mayan Factor.

Let's just say for now, as a cosmic ingredient, the Mayan Factor is the seasoning in your recipe for synchronicity. It is what puts the view back into your deja vu! It is your return ticket on the Zuvuya, the memory hotline that rides you to your own dimensional double! It is a memory connection back to something you have never really forgotten.

I have found that by encountering and playing with Uncle Joe, my return ticket on the Zuvuya has indeed doubled my pleasure. Uncle Joe is so adventuresome and cosmically well-travelled that *Surfers of the Zuvuya* is only the beginning of what promises to be a never-ending story. But it is a never-ending story in which you and I and everybody else — including the Earth — become the actual heroes and heroines. The pages of this story are literally the days of our lives. And because

Uncle Joe is *multi*dimensionally hooked up, he is smarter than I, more far out, and at the same time infinitely more practical. As a result, this book is his show.

But who is this Uncle Joe? Jive-talking cosmic trickster, tongue-in-cheek dimensional surfer, riding a laugh into the place where my defenses are most obvious — it seems as if he is almost always ridiculing me. But it is the play and ridicule of one who loves and knows me so intimately and so well that he can take the liberties that he does with me. In fact, he needs to take those liberties; otherwise he would not be doing his job.

I suppose we could think of Uncle Joe as my higher self. But in this case my higher self, my dimensional double, is out to clear away years of defensive pretentiousness in order to let the little boy in me come out and play. "Hey José, do you really need that Ph.D. after your name?" I can hear him asking me. But it is not just the little boy, it is the open, vulnerable heart that Uncle Joe is after. There is already too much seriousness without heart in this world. "What's wrong with playing a few jokes on God?" Uncle Joe says. "If you're really tuned into your dimensional double, you can play those jokes and still come out smelling like a rose!" And of course the little boy in me says, "Why not?"

As the story-telling tale-bearer of my larger, all-encompassing fourth dimensional being, there is never a time when Uncle Joe does not zap me. It is his Zuvuya zaniness that does it. He knows exactly how to crawl through the sewer lines of my ego and flush my conceptual expectations right into the cesspool of seedy ambitions and worn-out attitudes. What a guy!

Most of all, Uncle Joe is an expert on the infinite virtues of dwelling in the *now*. That is his place. That is where he hangs out. "Hang ten in the now," he says, "and that ever-loving galactic sea breeze will caress you forever!" And it's true. Whenever he ambushes me in of one of my funks, sooner than later I end up in the now with him. And I love it. You see, I have learned from Uncle Joe that it is from the wave crest of the now that you can set your sights on anything — and everything!

Though this work may read at times like a galactic fairy tale of one planet's quest for survival and the higher life, it is dead serious. Though some may dismiss it as sheer fantasy, I only speak what I believe, and I only believe what I have experienced. Everything I have experienced tells me that now is the time for right action on planet Earth. That is my pitch.

Uncle Joe agrees with my pitch. In fact, as I have learned, he is the one who has been pitching it. Our planet is in a jam, and ultimately there is only one purpose to lending your heart and energy towards riding the crest of the Zuvuya with us: to get us all moving!

According to the Mayan timetable, we have a five-year chasm to leap before we enter the twenty-year home stretch for this phase of evolution. In order to make it to the next evolutionary phase — post-2012 — we must create total world transformation. This transformation entails a revolution of attitude, a change unprecedented in human history!

Changes of this extraordinary nature are tricky business. Yet such changes can only be accomplished if people understand these changes in a joyous and happy manner. It will not work unless we play!

The importance of Uncle Joe's message is: *the world will only change once we accept and PLAY with the next dimension — the fourth-dimension!* In this regard, the radical worldview and the urgency of the message of *Surfers of the Zuvuya* builds on my previous work.

The appearance of Uncle Joe separates my new work from all of my previously published work. For this reason alone, it has been a distinct delight to write and present *Surfers of the Zuvuya*. This encounter with my dimensional double has affected me profoundly. It is my "coming out of the closet!" I hope that you will be equally affected by, and intrigued about, your own dimensional double.

In addition to taking you on an interdimensional voyage, it is my desire that this book will provoke you to consider your own life, and your own death. May the tale I have woven from the experience of my life and the death of my son be an inspiration for you to take into account the intensity of our times. And having taken these times into account, may you move lightly and playfully with the reality of your own double as your guide. May the greater mystery and magic once known in the hearts of all beings arouse again this wondrous planet, spaceship Earth, to its true destiny. Surf's up!

JOSÉ ARGÜELLES, Ph.D., Surfer of the Zuvuya
Boulder, Colorado
10 Akbal 9 Mac
April 1, 1988

1
THE
GREAT MAYAN
ENGINEERING TEAM & ITS
GALACTIC ESCAPADES

I am eager to get us introduced to my Uncle Joe, but first we must have some context, and some background. So we are going to set the stage. After all, Uncle Joe isn't just any old surfer — he is a *Mayan* surfer.

Everyone wants to know about the Maya. Who were they? Where did they come from? Where did they go? What did this ancient people and their calendar have to do with Harmonic Convergence, the greatest grassroots event in recent history?

There are still many Mayan people living today in the Yucatan, Southern Mexico, Guatemala, Honduras, and Belize. It is dangerous country. I get letters from long-lost friends living down there who tell me that the Day Keepers, the modern Maya who still keep up with the Tzolkin or Sacred Calendar, are getting their tongues pulled out by the mercenary armies that rule that part of the world. What can Harmonic Convergence mean to them, my friends? I wonder. You probably do too.

You probably have also seen or heard of the pyramids and the mysterious ruins in the jungles. And you may have heard that the Maya sacrificed children and tore people's hearts out after some bloody ball game. What is the real story behind all this?

If you fly down to Villahermosa, the oil capital of Mexico, you can rent a car and be at a place called Palenque in four hours. As Mayan ruins go, it is fairly accessible. And it is pure magic. Fantastic stone towers and temples peep up from the dense jungle, where monkeys and birds make all sorts of noise. Occasionally a wild boar breaks through the underbrush, snorting and pawing, with no manners at all.

The guidebook tells you about the nine-leveled Temple of the Inscriptions, dedicated in 683 AD. It also tells you that there is a tomb within the pyramid which was completed nine years later, in 692 AD. And, the guidebook says, a man named Pacal Votan was buried there.

The tomb is even more mysterious than the ruins outside. It is the only one like it in the New World. The only other thing close to it, New World or Old, is the tomb in the Great Pyramid of Cheops in Egypt. But, the guidebook tells you, a body was found in the Palenque tomb, while no body was found in the Great Pyramid.

To get to the tomb of Pacal Votan, you first climb up to the temple on top of the Pyramid. Then you go down narrow stairs. It is dank and dark. Finally you get to the tomb room. An ancient stone door has obviously been pulled open with great effort, like in the movie "Raiders of the Lost Ark." An eerie feeling comes over you. Will the tomb ever be closed again? "Ohmigod!" you think. "What *does* this mean?"

Peering through the bars, your eyes make out a large stone that is about twelve feet long and eight feet wide. It is the coffin lid. There, carved on this huge slab of limestone, is a man who seems to be sitting on a beast with a tree growing out of him. What is he doing? Is the giant beast beneath him going to swallow him whole? Is that a tree growing out of his solar plexus? Is he driving a spaceship? What is the scoop? As you puzzle over this thing, you get a chill. The hair on the back of your head stands on end. A spaceship? Are these Mayans from outer space?

The answer is a resounding *yes!* But nothing to fear. Most of us, at one time or another and in one form or another, came from outer space. More of that later. For now, let's stick with the ancient Maya, the ones who built Palenque: Pacal Votan and his cohorts. I think of them as the great Mayan engineering team: Galactic Scouts with a mission. And what was their mission? To make sure that planets and star systems are synchronized with the *galactic beam*.

But what is this *galactic beam* and what do the ancient Maya have to do with it? And how do I know all this?

I don't blame you for getting perplexed. Just catch your breath and I will explain some things for you.

The truth is, although I still go to supermarkets and raise kids who give me a run for my money by imitating what's happening on MTV rock videos, I am a Mayan. If you see a picture of me, you will say: "That guy looks more like my Uncle Charlie than a Mayan!" And that may be true. But I have learned how to live like a Mayan. I have learned how to do that by remembering not only who I am now, but who and where I have been in the past, and even who I might become in the future! And I have learned to live on Mayan time, even though I seem to be just like everybody else. Before you say "preposterous!" just listen to my story.

You can call me Joe Zuvuya if you want. That's actually the name of my uncle who lives in the next dimension over. But because I am a Mayan, I can also be my uncle. I will explain that later when I tell you how the *Zuvuya* works.

Right now all you need to know is that the *Zuvuya* is a memory hotline. It circulates the memories you need for whatever situation comes up. Not only that, the Zuvuya accesses memories just as easily from the past as from the future. The Zuvuya is not just for Mayans, either. Anyone can hook up to it. It is like free energy. It is there all the time.

Don't worry or be threatened by my suggestions. I am still wet behind the ears myself because I only hooked up to the Zuvuya a few years ago. I am still learning how to ride it. But I have discovered that the real key is trust, and radical surrender.

When I first started exercising with the Zuvuya, I travelled a lot on airplanes. You are between one place and another when you are flying, just as when you use the Zuvuya you are between one time and another. Similarly, it is good to practice with the Zuvuya when you take a siesta, because during a siesta you do not really sleep. You hang out between the dimensions: between the physical plane and the dream world. The physical location of your body also holds you in your own dimension, so you can move to another more easily when you travel.

One trip out of Indianapolis a couple of years ago, I was up at 35,000 feet, doing my siesta and catching the Zuvuya. Suddenly a voice came on inside of my head and said, "OK, you're riding it good. Now you get a little reward. What do you want? Who do you want to hook up with? You only get one shot, so think about it."

Gadzooks! One shot.

Well, fresh from a trip to Palenque, there was no question that I wanted a direct line to Pacal Votan.

"You got it," the voice came back. I was on.

Pacal Votan knocked my socks off. So did his wife, his galactic teammate, Ah Po Hel. She was actually the one who later filled me in on the beam.

"Galactic Agent 13 66 56, a.k.a. Pacal Votan, coming through. Do you hear me?"

I heard him loud and clear.

"What do you want to know? What do you want to talk about?"

"Simple," I replied. "Were you guys from outer space or what?"

"Good question! We were wondering when you'd get serious and ask the right question. Isn't it obvious to you that we came from somewhere else? What other reason would we have had to create what you think of as the most incredible and accurate calendar ever devised? But that's the problem. You thought all those numbers were calendar markings and that we drove ourselves nuts carving huge calendar stones every 5, 10, or 20 years! Who would want to do that? No way! We weren't keeping a calendar like everyone thinks. We were making sure that Earth was synchronizing with the galactic beam. We're synchronic engineers! Get with the program, guy!"

Well, not wanting to be thought of as a guy who was out of it, a guy who was not with the program, I got with the program. And this is what I learned.

First of all, Pacal Votan, who lived on this planet between 631 and 683 AD, came here as the chief of a crack Mayan galactic engineering team. But he was not the first Mayan to get to this planet. The first Mayan, at least of his particular team, came a lot earlier — maybe close to 1300 years earlier — around 600 BC. But long, long before that, the Maya had been surveying our planet, watching it. Why? Well, as Pacal Votan put it to me, higher evolution on Earth had gotten off to a shaky start. This was due to the imprinting of the genetic circuits, the DNA, the biological microchips, the stuff we are made of. Pacal also gave me information about Atlantis. But we will get to that later, too.

The Maya knew that about 5100 years ago our planet entered the critical phase of a galactic beam. These galactic beams are of all kinds and they originate in the center of the galaxy, which the Maya call Hunab Ku. The Hunab Ku is like a great powerful radio station which sends out all these beams, each beam having a different program. Apparently, the farther out you get the wider the beam becomes. Possibly it weakens. I found this fascinating!

The beams interact with and evolve the stuff of life so that evolution, at whatever level, can proceed at just the right rate, and everything stays as balanced as it can. Scientists, it seems, have just begun to notice some of these beams. They call them density waves because they tend to be of very low frequency, like gravity.

On our planet we hit a critical phase of this particular beam 5100 years ago, in 3113 BC to be exact. The beam's program was matched to the *frequency* of our advanced human DNA circuits. Our wiring was pretty fancy then, and still is, but it is a little screwed up. The effect of this beam matching with our genetic programming was — zap! — to create what we call recorded history.

Because of my own studies, I was amazed. It is a fact that, in 3113 BC, Menes, the first pharaoh, was unifying upper and lower Egypt and setting up the *first* recorded historical dynasty. But then that was the way the Maya set it up. That is why their job in the galaxy is to be synchronic engineers: the team who makes sure that things on any planet or star occur in synch with the program of the beams focussed on them from galactic center, for whatever phase of evolutionary development. It seems obvious that there are other beams they work with, but this was Earth's beam, and its timing exactly matched the human historic cycle of the last 5100 years!

The effect of this beam, 5125 Earth years wide, was to help accelerate human activity around the planet. This acceleration is called recorded history. When the planet phases out of the beam — which it will do around 2012 AD — the plan is that humans *should* have created a unified global civilization living in harmony with nature. This would help humans and the planet be ready for the next evolutionary cycle.

Of course, some places need more help than others. And our little planet, which we would love to believe is the garden spot of the universe, happens to be one of those places. What the Maya knew was that, while the beam had the correct program for this critical phase of development, the human genetic circuits were just a little out of phase.

Incidentally, the Maya call this beam an "acceleration-synchronization beam." First it accelerates human activity, causing an interesting side effect: material technology. Towards the end of the beam, acceleration is supposed to become exponential. Population explodes, technology is everywhere, and the stock market cannot stop going straight up the charts. When it becomes absolutely exponential, acceleration is supposed to phase into synchronization. That is when every-body starts to say to everybody else: "Hey! did you notice *that!*" And everyone says *that* all at the same time. Is that coincidence or ESP? Who can tell for sure? Synchronization is fun, but very intense!

For the first half of the beam, the first 2600 years or so, the mismatching between the beam program and the faulty human genetic circuits was not that noticeable, at least if you were watching the planet from a spaceship. But it was always there. The Christians came to call it "original sin," while over in India they said "bad karma." Also during the first 2600 years, the Babylonians hassled people in the Middle East for quite a few centuries, only to be knocked out by an even more aggressive group called the Persians. The Egyptians and the Chinese tried to keep an even keel with powerful successions of royal dynasties. The Greeks began to build beautiful little temples on cliffs above the Aegean sea, while the Druids in the British Isles made offerings by moonlight in eery sanctuaries like Stonehenge.

Scouts from the Mayan galactic engineering team knew that midway through the beam things would pick up speed. Whatever had been set in motion would accelerate into an increasing phase of warlike empire expansion in what we now call the Old World — Northern Africa, Asia and Europe. For this reason, in 550 BC — precisely midpoint in the beam — the Maya sent down one of their top people. They even included a clue to his identity. This person, Prince Siddhartha, later called Gautama the Buddha, had a mother named *Maya*.

In a world increasingly given over to greed, ambition, and power, the Buddha came to remind people of compassion and the true nature of wisdom, which he said you could get by quieting your mind. Wandering around India with his begging bowl, the former prince was proficient at disarming worldly souls. As a result, after he ended his worldly life and entered *nirvana*, the followers of the Buddha formed a religion. It was the first *historical* religion, a religion based on the teachings of someone who had become dissatisfied with the process of human history.

While the Buddha was good for spreading a calming influence as things began to speed up in the Old World, the Mayan Scouts said, "Well, we're still going to have to make a genetic model and implant a whole group of people so that later we can send down our crack engineering team to do the fine-tuning for this planet."

Infiltrating planets is no easy matter, because there are cosmic laws about entering other dimensions. One basic cosmic law states that you cannot interfere with the evolutionary destiny of others. This means you cannot impose your will on another's will. You cannot just land your UFO on the White House lawn and say, "We're here! Quit polluting the planet and making nuclear weapons!" That may have worked for Hitler, and then for him only for a little while, but it doesn't work for Mayans.

Another cosmic law says: "Honor the intelligence!" This means that everyone has natural wisdom, and if you want to understand folks, check them out first and go with their flow. Finally, there is the nitty gritty of the galactic code of honor. It is the Mayan saying, *In Lake'ch*, "I am another yourself." If you live by that one, even though you may get in over your head in some things — screwed over by one of your buddies, for instance — you can get out of another dimension without killing yourself or your neighbor. That is important, because when a planet is infiltrated, the ones who come down from space do not want to add to the planet's karma. That would be totally counterproductive.

Given all these considerations, and given that the planet was midpoint in the beam 2500 to 2600 years ago, the Mayan Scouts figured out that the best place to create a genetic model and to do an implant was not in the Old World, because there was too much going on there. They would get noticed too easily. They would be thought of as weird, and would probably be killed for that reason alone. No, that certainly would not do.

But over in the New World things were a little different, a little slower, a little more predisposed to a Mayan implant. There in the jungles around the gulf of Mexico, extending down through the mountain highlands of Central America, was a perfect spot. The people there were not going around killing each other — yet. There was one group called the Olmecs, the Rubber People, and another group called the

Zapotecs, the Cloud People. These groups were into farming and making art out of stone and jade and beautiful woven things. They were also into magic mushrooms, which they called, for good reason, "flesh of the gods."

The Mayan Scouts realized that if you want to check out the dynamic nature of your relationship to the universe, and how this actually works through your senses, you should eat some of these mushrooms, sit on top of a mountain, and see how it goes. The web of creation. The original universe network. The ethics of deep ecology revealed: you are it. It is you. Flesh of the gods. They said it was a way to feel the vibrations of the galactic core, Hunab Ku, while still living on Earth.

"Cosmically inclined all the way!" was the Mayan Scouts' assessment of these Olmecs and Zapotecs, the Rubber People and the Cloud People. "They talk to the trees, they talk to the jaguars, they listen to the clouds, they put their ears to the stars. People like that won't be at all surprised if a few of us come down from the mountains, grow corn like them, weave like them, eat mushrooms, and show them a little device we use that we call the Tzolkin, the galactic constant. We'll tell them it's a perpetual 260-day calendar, a sacred calendar that interfaces with their solar calendar every 52 years. Great!"

So the Maya implanted a unique genetic model, but one that was close enough to the models around them that it was hard to tell the difference. Following the galactic code of Hunab Ku, the Maya divided into thirteen tribes of seven warrior clans each, which infiltrated the dense jungles and mountain highlands. Within a few centuries everybody was using the 260-day calendar. That was when the people in that part of the world really started to hit their stride.

In Central Mexico, by the third century BC, they began to build a place called Teotihuacan, "place where the gods touch the Earth." This was the main center. It was not Mayan, exactly. But then it was. There was enough of the Mayan juice in it to make it a favorite spot for the Galactic Scouts, who visited it·often.

By the time Jesus Christ was born — he was the second one to come down into the Old World to remind everybody about peace and love and doing "his father's work" — Teotihuacan had 200,000 residents. Interesting that the Pyramid of the Sun at Teotihuacan has almost the same base measurement as the Great Pyramid at Egypt, because by 0 AD the ancient Mexicans and the New World were ready to start their acceleration process with great intensity, just as the Egyptians had begun their acceleration process in the Old World when the Great Pyramid was built.

At the same time that Teotihuacan was built in Central Mexico, the Maya built their first big center in Guatemala. El Mirador, it is called today, meaning "the look-out." And look-out it was! Here the Maya sent up a signal. Everything was going according to schedule. A Mayan base camp had been established, and the Scouts were being called Mayan on Earth. The Maya had given enough influence to the surrounding cultures to help boost them into high civilization, yet without dominating them. Because of this, these cultures could be counted on to remain tolerant and receptive to whatever other Mayan activity might occur.

Now Mayans, as you might have gathered, are patient. They are also masters of time and illusion — magicians, if you will. And, as synchronic engineers, they know their beams. Knowing their beams, they know the most appropriate time for action and the most appropriate time for withdrawal or retreat.

Back to the beam. The beam of critical importance that we are passing through, the one that we entered in 3113 BC, consists of thirteen large frequency cycles called *baktuns*.

Each frequency cycle or baktun is like a radio program. It has its own unique quality and is also affected by the previous cycles. Each baktun cycle lasts a little over 394 Earth years, and each one has a special evolutionary program. The thirteen large frequency cycles are illustrated and explained in *The Mayan Factor*. We are currently in the last one, the thirteenth baktun, the one that ends in 2012 AD. The baktun which the Buddha came into was the seventh cycle, Baktun 6. Christ was at the tail end of the eighth cycle, Baktun 7.

During Baktun 8, 41-435 AD, the Mayans in Central America realized they had to get serious. The perfect — and only — time to give the planet a complete tune-up and synchronize it totally with the beam was the tenth cycle, Baktun 9, which on our calendar was 435-830 AD. In the middle of this baktun, another Galactic Scout infiltrated Earth: Muhammed. He had the toughest job, actually, because he had to work in the place where the karma had gotten most screwed up: the Middle East.

In any case, because of all the factors involved, such as duration of beam, accumulated effect of acceleration, beam program in relation to genetic program — it was clear that Baktun 9 was the ideal frequency cycle of the beam for the crack Mayan galactic engineering team to do its tune-up job. Their directions were, "Hit the planet with your top beam squad. Take resonant frequency measurements. Engage in psychic and ritual attunement with the planetary field. Let the galactic program run its cycle, and hope for the best so that sometime in the future when things have calmed down, you can do a return engagement!"

Suddenly, in places like Tikal and Copan, they appeared. Disguised as clever, late Stone Age artists and sun worshippers, the engineering team took readings on the galactic frequencies as measured through sunspot cycles. The crack

Mayan engineering team then put their records on great
stone monuments which the archeologists today call *stelae*.
Naturally, all the markings take as their point of reference
the Earth's entry into this beam back in 3113 BC.

When the team had gotten an accurate reading of the
planet in relation to the beam, and to the other planets of
the solar system, their chief came down to survey the job.
That was Pacal Votan, and the year was 631 AD. He set
up court at Palenque and also traveled around a bit to see
how things were going. Being quite the magician as well,
he loved entertaining at his court. You would be surprised
who showed up there. Merlin was a favorite, along with
some other magicians from China, Java, and India. Ah Po
Hel, the Chief Lady of the Court of Palenque, put on quite
a spread. Everyone enjoyed themselves. It was not a bad
time on the planet. Even the Germanic tribes had begun
to settle down in Europe, while in the Middle East the
followers of Muhammed had begun to reshape the ancient
cradle of civilization.

When Pacal Votan's "tomb" was completed in 693 AD,
there were exactly seven *katun* cycles, or cycles of about
twenty years, left to close out Baktun 9. Twenty katuns
make one baktun. If a baktun is similar to a whole radio
program, then the katuns could be compared to segments
of the program between the ads. Since there are thirteen
baktuns to the beam cycle that runs from 3113 BC to 2012
AD, there are a total of 260 (13x20) katuns to this same
beam cycle. You will notice that there are as many katuns
in this cycle, called the Great Cycle, as there are days in
the Sacred Calendar. That is because 260 is the galactic
constant. I will say more on that later, because the Mayans
had the most accurate numerical system ever known.

It was during these last seven katun cycles, or seven
generations, of Baktun 9 — 692-830 AD — that the crack

Mayan galactic engineering team went to town. They wailed. Planet Earth was receiving a tune-up. She was being placed in attunement with resonant transmitter-receivers in far-flung time/space points of the galaxy. This attunement activity was especially intense at Copan and its allied center, Quirigua, both in Honduras.

If you go to Copan and Quirigua, as well as to Coba up near Tulum, you will find dates — the Maya call them calibrations — that anchor us into the deep past. On Stela D at Quirigua there are two dates: one 411,683,935 years ago, another 873,600,000 years ago. On Stela F at Quirigua is a date 1,193,600,000 years into the past. Another glyph, the Mecham glyph, records a date 25,600,000,000 years in the past. Still another, the Mukulmam glyph, records a date 10,240,000,000,000 years ago! That is so far back it's probably in the future!

Larry Tyler, a Mayan "cycleologist," thinks these dates have to do with key moments in the creation of life in the universe. The oldest date would correspond to the pinpoint emergence of the super Hunab Ku, the infinitesimal creative center from which this universe and all entire universes have emerged — and returned.

Quirigua was the place where the galactic engineering team had its final gathering at the end of Baktun 9 in 830 AD. They thanked the Mayan people, descendents of the first implant, for their hospitality and graciousness. They admonished them to stay calm, to go back to the jungle, and to live a simple life. Why? Because the acceleration cycles were only to bring greater and greater trouble to this planet.

Soon would come the warlords, and after them, conquerors who were ever more ruthless, powerful, and devastating. And even after them, long into the future, almost until the end of the entire Great Cycle, barbarian mercenaries called

Spaniards would terrorize their descendents, tearing out
their tongues and destroying their villages. Later in the last
baktun, other intruders would despoil the jungles with their
machines and guerilla armies. But when that happened,
it would be known: the Great Cycle was about to come
to an end.

In 830 AD, the engineering team departed back to space,
back to the other dimensions from which the Maya keep
their watch on things. Slowly the terrestrial Maya melted
back into the jungles. The time of darkness was setting in.
Sure enough the conquerors came. By 830 AD Teotihuacan
had already been sacked. Warrior tribes who took the ancient
name of Toltec, which means Master Builders, entered the
Yucatan. War and human sacrifice were introduced.

Then, because the people of the Earth had begun to
forget about peace, harmony, and divine revelation, which
they had learned from the Buddha, Christ, and Muhammed,
another man was sent down, this time in the New World.
This was Quetzalcoatl, called by the Maya, Kukulkan. He
lived 52 years, like Pacal Votan, between 947 and 999 AD.
He had the same thankless task as his predecessors: teach
the people to love one another, to live in peace, and to be
grateful. They will probably listen and then betray you. Oh
yes, and one other thing. Before you sail away on your raft
of serpents, do not forget to leave them the prophecies.

Ah, the prophecies! There were to be thirteen heavens
and nine hells, and each was to be a cycle of 52 years. The
first heaven began in 843 AD following the thirteen "dead
years" after the departure of the great engineering team.
Quetzalcoatl's life spanned the third of these heaven cycles.
The thirteenth heaven cycle would end in 1519, and then
would follow the nine hell cycles.

In fact, the first of the nine hell cycles began precisely
the day Cortes set foot on Mexican soil, at a place now

known as Vera Cruz, or True Cross. Of course, much to
the dismay of the Christian priests, one of the symbols
of Quetzalcoatl was also a cross. "How did that cross get
here?" they thought, furious and chagrined.

The ninth hell cycle ended August 16, 1987, at Harmonic
Convergence. You may wonder if Quetzalcoatl/Kukulkan
could have envisioned that his prophecy would have been
celebrated by so many people who had hardly ever heard
of him, much less pronounce his name. But that is the way
of the Maya — it seeps in everywhere, like a mist rolling
through a forest.

From the point of view of the Mayan engineering team
that was monitoring this whole spectacle the next dimension
over, along with my Uncle Joe Zuvuya, Harmonic Convergence was on the beam! The human population had peaked
at over five billion. The stock market was zooming upwards,
and headed for a crash. Technology and materialism had
conquered the world. Acceleration had reached exponential
proportions. The timing was exquisite.

And, as if responding to a signal in their genetic programming, thousands of humans responded to the call of
Harmonic Convergence. Return to the Earth — make peace
with nature! But only 25 years to achieve this before the
end of the beam in 2012? Can it really be done? As the
Maya know, time will tell!

My Uncle Joe Zuvuya tells me that the Mayan engineering
team is anxious for this cycle to close out properly. What
does that mean? Well, this 5125-year beam is actually the
last fifth of a beam that is close to 26,000 years wide. This
big 26,000-year beam corresponds to a whole evolutionary
phase. Our current evolutionary phase is called *Homo sapiens*
because *Homo sapiens* emerged during the ice age, 26,000
years ago, at the beginning of the beam. *Homo sapiens*
means clever humans. Our civilization is the materialistic

acme of *Homo sapiens'* cleverness. You can't beat what we've done. And if we keep on doing it, there'll be nothing left to beat, and the joke will be on us.

From the perspective of the Galactic Scouts, we humans are like massive addicts. We are addicted to chemicals and artificial stimulants of all kinds, and just about everything we do produces toxic waste. The Galactic Scouts laugh at us because we cannot see that we are the cancer of the Earth. They laugh because we cannot see that it is all connected: radioactivity, carbon monoxide pollution, cancer, AIDs, the depleting ozone layer, the dying dolphins, the disappearing rain forest, terrorism, the increasing cloud cover — it is all one piece, an expression of our collective addictions.

The root of the problem is materialistic greed, which is really one-dimensional fixation. We are the monkey on Earth's back, but Earth wants to kick her habit. "Humans," she says, "you'd better look out, 'cuz mama's gonna shake and your back is gonna break!"

Harmonic Convergence was very Mayan. It demonstrated our understanding that the only way to peace is through returning to the Earth, and through re-establishing harmony with nature. The Earth is alive. It is nature. It is greater and wiser than us. It bred us. It contains us. And if necessary, it will destroy us. If we return to the Earth, why should we worry? The Earth has always cooperated in evolving ever-higher forms of life. Why don't we rejoin the show, and get back to the evolutionary mainstream? It could be a lot more fun than we are having now.

Harmonic Convergence demonstrated that there are still enough humans with enough willpower — if only for two days — to show that they are willing to kick the habit. But can they follow through? Can the people who did Harmonic Convergence become Mayan enough to lead the way back to the evolutionary mainstream?

According to Uncle Joe, in 2012 we will hit an evolutionary juncture when we will have new possibilities. We will get funded on the spot to develop a new improved model of ourselves — *Homo terrestrialis* — Earth human, human in cooperation with the Earth. And, as an added bonus, this new planetary human will be endowed with galactic consciousness.

The trick to getting ourselves refunded is simple: it is the flip of the switch that takes us from our locked-in, materialistic, third-dimensional reality to a recognition that we are multidimensional beings in a multidimensional universe! But before we get funded, we have to wake up and clean up our act! Clean up time and fast!

My Uncle Joe also tells me that we can get help, but only if we want it. In addiction, the addict has to come to the point where he or she knows that outside help is necessary if the habit is going to be kicked. There is too much arrogance and too much self-deception in doing it alone. Do you want help? Are you ready? Even if you are not, the Galactic Scouts are. What do you say?

Remember: for the Mayan engineers, this planet is another project, a galactic escapade, a planetary thriller. They are rooting for us. What we do not understand is how big the stakes are. Our ball of wax is connected to parts of the universe we never dreamed of, and if it blows, the shakedown goes all the way.

Then let's get on with it. This is the entrance to the big circuit, the grand Zuvuya. It's all for you and it's all about you. And it's all about time. And the time is now. All you have to do is learn how to become a Mayan like my Uncle Joe. We can pay him a visit right now.

2
HOW TO
RIDE THE ZUVUYA
& BECOME A MAYAN

 Now that I have introduced you to the Mayans, not just as builders of pyramids in the jungles, but as Galactic Scouts and synchronic engineers, let's go meet one of these Mayans. Obviously they are playful. They get around. They are discreet, too.

How do we locate a Mayan? We locate a Mayan the same way they get around. And how do they get around? They ride the Zuvuya.

Zoo-vu-yah! It's not hard to pronounce. Or if you want, Zoo-vu-yeah! Remember how we defined it? A memory circuit hotline. Now let's try to understand that. What is a memory circuit hotline? For starters, let's begin with deja vu.

Everyone has had a deja-vu experience. You are at the drinking fountain, just leaning down to glurp a sip of water, hoping you won't splash it all over your make-up. But you do. Why? Because just as you were about to put your lips to the stream of water, a funny thing hit you. Where had you seen this fountain before? Was it really a fountain, or was it a waterfall? And someone was standing there saying

something, saying something to you about ... remembering
... to remember?

And then you can't tell whether this moment now at
the drinking fountain is actually the memory, or whether
the memory is actually the reality. That's it! Reality is the
dream! Memory is the reality! Just as you try to squeeze back
into the reality of the waterfall, which is more real than the
drinking fountain — poof! You are slightly disoriented. The
water is hitting your chin, not your mouth, and your boy-
friend is over in the corner snickering at you.

OK, you get the picture. Deja vu means that what you
are doing now you have already done before, in some other
time, in some other place. But it also feels like this current
reality is no less or no more real than the memory reality.
Conclusion: there is more than one reality!

Of course, somewhere deep inside of yourself you know
that. For instance, every night you go to sleep, and you
dream. Even if you do not remember your dreams, you still
dream. There is your physical body, lying down curled up
beneath the covers. But then, there is this *other* you, off
cavorting ... looking for the waterfall!

As you have probably noticed, things happen differently
in dreams. Faces melt. Waterfalls *do* become drinking foun-
tains. You meet people you never met before. It is not at
all real, at least not by your everyday waking standards.
And yet it feels *so* real. You wake up with a start — did
that just happen?

Could it be that the reality of the dream and the reality
of the deja vu are connected?

Let's bring up one more example: the premonition, or
what my fancy psychologist friends call the precognitive
experience. How does it happen that as you are doing the
ironing your brother's face comes to you, as clearly as if he
were right in front of you, and it feels to you like there is

something wrong. What is that about?

Later that afternoon, you hear from Mom that your brother was in a skiing accident, a thousand miles away. Don't worry, he's alright. He'll just be on crutches for awhile. When did that happen, you ask? And you learn that it was about the time you were doing your ironing. The theme music from "The Twilight Zone" dances eerily through your thoughts.

So now we have deja vus, dreams, premonitions, and ... synchronicity. Have you noticed that there is an extra charge in the air when you and your friend think the same thought and then say it at the same time? Both of your faces look awestruck and your eyes turn up to make sure no one is there. It is not just a question of another reality, but maybe ... of another yourself.

So what does all this have to do with the Zuvuya?

We live in a culture that usually says pooh-pooh to all this stuff. If you think about it, you are weird. You probably *buy* the *National Enquirer* rather than just reading it while standing in the supermarket line. But think of all the people who have these same experiences every day, day in and day out. What is going on?

Someone is not letting the cat out of the bag. You have these different kinds of experiences, and quite often at that. And it seems like they are connected — that there is synchronicity — but no one is letting on. No one is telling you what this is all about. They are not teaching "Deja Vu 101" at school. Are you being kept in the dark about this, and if so, why?

Before we get too conspiratorial, let's go check this out with my Uncle Joe. He is my fourth dimensional double, and he can see things easily since he is not in the third dimension like you and me.

First, though, let me tell you how Uncle Joe came into

my life.

For a long time I was like you, living my physical, third-dimensional life, being popped and ransacked by random deja vus, dreams, premonitions, and synchronicities. But then, as I told you in the last chapter, I came across the Zuvuya. At first it was just another word, another idea. But it haunted me.

The archeologists describe it as the "secret language" which the ancient Mayan wizards used when they talked about what happened or what was going to happen. When you read the language of the Zuvuya, it is like poetry, or the lyrics to some esoteric rock song. Intriguing, but not easily accessible. It is a language that is always emerging or receding, like the clouds, instead of simply being present.

Then I met Hunbatz Men. He is a real Mayan. Hunbatz was giving a lecture on Mayan astrology in a Washington elementary school classroom in Boulder, Colorado. He was dressed in white and wore a headband, on the front of which was a circle that enclosed a square tipped on its corner. Hunbatz declared that the Zuvuya is the circuit by which everything returns to itself. That is a metaphysical cruncher. Another way you could say this is that everything is the memory of itself.

What this means is that your location in the present moment, any present moment, is in the center of an infinity loop: a figure 8 on its side. The future is one loop; the past is the other loop. Since these memory loops are continuously in motion, what you are in the present moment is being continously defined by the memories that are meeting in that present moment: the center cross-point of the figure 8.

If you are a functioning Mayan, then the past and the future are continuously circulating their memories to you — and you are conscious of it. Most of the time however, you may not be aware and so you are not at the center. You are someplace else, thinking about the car in the garage, or whether your kids are doing well in school, or whether you are going to get that job promotion or not.

These kinds of thoughts, which are happening most of the time, with little break between them, are like sandbags pushed up against the portals to the memory hotline, the Zuvuya. Except, that is, when some little break occurs such as the random deja vu, the premonition, or the synchronicity.

I started working with the Zuvuya, getting myself to center, and trying to balance my awareness at that teeny weeny spot where the infinity loops run into each other. Tuning in. That was when Uncle Joe appeared.

Every one of you has voices inside your head. Among all the voices in your head, there is one voice that is truer than all the other voices. This is the voice of your intuition, your higher self, your higher power. People used to say that it was your conscience. What is this intuition, that would cause it to have a voice?

From the Mayan point of view, intuition is the activity of the memory hotline, the Zuvuya. The voice in *my* head that I finally tracked down was the voice of Uncle Joe: Joe Zuvuya.

"You wanna know something?" he said, startling me in the midst of one of my siestas.

"Who are you?" I asked, recognizing the voice as the oldest one I had ever known or could remember. In this moment, though, it was as if I was hearing the voice for the first time.

"I'm your dimensional double, Uncle Joe Zuvuya." This announcement made me feel uneasy, as if someone was playing a trick on me. Yet, at the same time that I experienced this perspiration-evoking uneasiness, I felt amazingly tuned in. "OK," I thought to myself, taking a very deep breath, "whatever Don Juan, trickster, coyote thing this might be, I'm ready!"

"Dimensional double?" I asked him. "What do you mean dimensional double?"

"First of all, Bud, there are some things you should learn if you're going to go around doing the things you do and saying the things you say," he replied. Even though his manner smacked of cosmic jive, I could tell he was serious.

"OK, talk to me," I said, relaxing into what I figured would be an interesting discussion. "Tell me about the dimensional double." Here is what my Uncle Joe Zuvuya told me.

Every single one of us is born with a dimensional double which is kind of like the soul, or the higher or better self. But it is not just an image. The dimensional double is real.

The way to understand it is this: the body you look at and see in the mirror is your third-dimensional body. The third dimension is the physical plane. The physical plane consists of everything you can weigh and measure and buy for your house. Science deals only with that level. It is everything you touch, taste, smell, hear, and see. Even all of the fine precision instruments that science uses still don't get out of the physical plane, the third dimension. So everything you know about and everything you're taught about as real is just this feedback from our third-dimensional, physical plane world.

Obviously, there are other dimensions.

The dimensional double is in the fourth dimension, the next dimension over. It is there all the time, trying to give your third-dimensional being information that might help it, if the third-dimensional being is ready to hear it. All those synchronicities, deja vus, and premonitions, as well as all those dreams — that's your fourth-dimensional double doing its number — trying to get you to pay attention.

"What do you look like, Uncle Joe? Do you have a body?" I asked him, appreciative of all of this information.

"For you, I look kind of like a Mayan version of yourself, except that my molecules are spread out and vibrate at a frequency at least ten times faster than your third-dimensional molecules," he answered with great patience.

"What's your role, Uncle Joe? What are you here for and what are you doing for me?"

"Now we're getting down to it, Bud," he answered with what was certainly a well-deserved familiarity.

"I'm your memory circuit, hotline keeper, your Zuvuya keeper. I'm the one who keeps the score on what you're up to. You see, I've got an investment in you. Not only do I keep your account, but I'm interested in seeing to it that you stay on course, because by staying on your course I get greater returns on my investment. I'm also the one who sees to it that whatever information I can get from upstairs gets to you. But you've got to keep the lines open at all times, or else it's just a wasted effort."

"What do you mean you've got an investment in me?" I asked, slightly insulted that Uncle Joe thought of me as some kind of commodity.

"Ruffled your feathers, huh?" I could hear him chuckling. "My investment in you is this: we're in this together. You're my third-dimensional property. But I'm only as good as you are clear. The more clear you get about your intentions on this planet, the more light I can pour into you; the more light I can pour into you, the easier you make my job."

"Well, what's your job, Uncle Joe?" I was getting intrigued.

"My job is to see to it that when you've run your course, when you're ready to turn in your body, that you and I have our two-way communication so clear that we're totally clean. The sooner and the more harmonically we can converge when you die — when your body gives out — the better.

Because then it's *our* choice what happens next and where
we go, get it? We could even harmonically converge now and
be ahead of the game! That's why I said it's so important
for you to stay on your course."

"But, Uncle Joe, what do you mean by my course?"

"That's simple, Bud. Your course is staying in your
integrity."

"That's easy to say. But what is my integrity really?"

"Your integrity is the sum total of all of your imperfections . . ."

"My imperfections?" I cut Uncle Joe off, blustering and
not a little insulted.

"Yes, your imperfections. Because they are what you're
trying to hide all the time. And when you're trying to hide
them, well, you're not you. You're not in your truth. You're
not in your integrity.

"See, the great irony is this: each one of us alone is
nothing and everything. We're nothing because obviously
there's more to the whole entire universe than us. We're not
even a speck on a fly's rump compared to the rest of the
universe. And yet, we're all we know.

"You see, all we know about the universe comes through
our infinitesimally minute being. And this being itself, with
its warts and all, is our gift. It's our existence itself. It's all
we have to give, and we shouldn't be ashamed of it. *You*
shouldn't be ashamed of it. When you're completely accepting
of yourself, then you're in your integrity. Then you can
exist. And if you can be fearless about it, then you can go
along on your path. Want to know something else?"

"What's that, Uncle Joe?"

"If it weren't for me, you wouldn't look like you do."

"Now wait a minute, Uncle Joe. I spend a lot of time
grooming myself, picking out my clothes, putting on my
style. What do you mean?"

"Well, it's like I said. You're my investment — my piece of real estate in the physical plane. When you're a good tenant, when you're in your integrity and clear about your intentions, then I get to put more into my investment. That gives you a certain light or charm. Sometimes it even translates as charisma. And when you're not a good tenant, then I withdraw my light — to let you know, even though you might not know it, that you're not being a good tenant. When I withdraw my light, then you appear dull and stupid."

"So are you a light being . . . a light body?"

"*Your* light being and *your* light body, Bud."

"That's cool. And everyone has one?"

"Yep. They sure do, although most people nowadays are only dimly aware of it. You might even call the dimensional double your dream body. It's what runs your errands when you dream. Or you could call it your guardian angel. Goes with the territory. Soon as you're born, it's born with you.

"It might seem that people who die accidental deaths do so because they are in disregard of their dimensional double, their guardian angel. But it might just be their double saying, 'Surprise! Accident's the teaching. We're done here now. Time to go elsewhere.' Fact is, the secret of the Maya is all in the light body. That's the keeper of the Zuvuya, remember? That's where this whole conversation started."

"Oh, yeah." I replied. "Tell me more about that. How does all this fit in with the Maya?"

"You see, the secret of the Maya is that they are riders of the Zuvuya."

"I like that, Uncle Joe. It's like a song: Riders of the Zuvuya."

"Riders of the Zuvuya, star dreamers punching prophecy through the holes in our conceptions . . ." Uncle Joe sang and giggled a little before continuing in his informative manner. "Right. The Maya were and are ahead of the game as far as you humans are concerned, because they're hooked up with their light bodies all the time. That means they're in synch with themselves, and they're as much in the future as they are in the past.

"What you humans have to do is get hooked up with your light bodies. That's a lot better than getting a new car or stereo anyday. That's because when you're hooked up with your light body, you can travel anywhere you want, you can hear anything you want, and you can see anything you want."

"C'mon, Uncle Joe. Isn't that a little far-fetched?" I nodded with some irritation.

"Far-fetched is right. Far out as well. But it's true. You see, you humans don't know the first thing about inter-dimensional play. That's why you're so bogged down. You only give credibility to one dimension — the third — when you've got the equipment to play with more — at least the fourth and the fifth."

"The fifth dimension! Tell me about that, Uncle Joe," I said, vaguely remembering a Woodstock-era rock group with that name.

"OK," he paused reflectively, and then continued. "Where I am there is still a world. It's like your world. It's got its own kind of substance, but it all moves at a faster rate of vibration. Besides guardian angels like me, the fourth dimension has its own population: fairies, and all sorts of what you call spirit beings. And it's much more fluid here in the fourth dimension. That's how I can get memories to you from either the past or the future. Information about things you wouldn't otherwise be able to get in contact with.

"But, I'm not at the top. Above me there's the fifth dimension. Beyond that, there are dimensions all the way up to the twelfth. Thirteen, if you throw in Hunab Ku.

Now the fifth dimension, that's the place where all the heavies hang out."

"The heavies?" I asked.

"Well," Uncle Joe chuckled again. "I should say the *lighties*. They're not heavy at all. They're pure electromagnetic vibration. You can't weigh that stuff."

"But who are the lighties then, Uncle Joe?"

"The lighties, they're the head honchos. As far as your planet is concerned, the lighties are the ones in charge of the planetary programs, the broadcasts they get directly from the Sun. Then the Sun gets its programs from some other stars, and also from galactic central, Hunab Ku. The important thing for you to understand is that the more clear you are with me, then the more I get from the lighties myself."

"OK, Uncle Joe," I answered. "You make the lighties sound like they're some kind of DJs or talk show hosts. But planetary programs from the Sun? What are you talking about, Uncle Joe?"

"Hey, we're really rolling now, aren't we? You know all the archaeologists think that people like the ancient Maya were into Sun worship. But the way the archaeologists describe Sun worship, it's like something superstitious. But that's because the archaeologists, just like the scientists, are seeing things only from this one dimension. I mean, wouldn't one of those archaeologists think you were a crackpot talking to me like this? See the problem?"

"No doubt about that, Uncle Joe," I replied. "But go on, tell me about the planetary programs from the Sun. What do they have to do with the Zuvuya? Is it like the Zuvuya is the circuit of all these dimensions you're describing?"

"OK. It's like here we get a broadcast from galactic central, Hunab Ku. It comes in streams and beams. It also comes in different dimensional bands. What are these broadcast beams — light waves, radio waves, gravity waves, and maybe even genetic information waves? All of these for sure.

"Well, all of these waves *are* information; they come *in* formation. Get it? Wherever there is another form with a similar wave frequency, these galactic Hunab Ku waves find their target. That's called resonance — a matching of wave formations. You know, Bud, you're a wave-form and you yourself resonate. That's got something to do with that integrity stuff we were talking about earlier, hee hee hee!"

Now I was getting impatient again. "Get back to the planetary programs and the Zuvuya, Uncle Joe!"

"Slow down, Bud. You *are* the planetary program from the Sun, and when you ride the Zuvuya, I mean really ride it, and not just dabble around with this synchronicity and deja vu stuff, you're processing the big circuit. You're getting into the memory bank in the sky. You're flying!"

"What do you mean that *I* am the planetary program from the Sun?"

"Get a clue, kid. Where do you think you came from? What do you think you are? I mean what are you really made of? What is your true nature? Did it ever occur to you that maybe you're a broadcast, a special service announcement meant to be played just for this time period?"

"Huh?" Uncle Joe was moving fast. I felt like I was losing my marbles. Whatever thoughts I had left were spilling out of my brains and rolling all over the floor in a spastic random manner.

"Relax, Bud. I don't mean to be getting you so fired up, if I may say so. But let's get this straight now. Biologically, you're the result of a particular set of DNA programs. This set of programs is your wave-form. This wave-form is unique because of its imperfectness which is the same as your integrity.

"And why is it a wave-form? Because DNA vibrates.

DNA has its own vibratory structure. It's a wave-form because you're also electromagnetic. Your nerve endings, your brainwaves, your ... radiance. You're a radiant guy, you know that? Thanks to me that is. I don't mean to steal your thunder, but the sooner you start owning up to *my* role in your affairs, the better off we'll both be. This is a win-win situation if there ever was one! If I win, you win; if you win, I win, and we all win together. Remember, you don't want to cross your dimensional double!

"OK. I know you're impatient, so it's like this. You're a wave-form. So is the planet. So is the Sun. You're on the Earth and of the Earth. You feel the glowing rays of the Sun. How could you be separate from the Earth and the Sun? You're not. Your wave-form and the Earth's wave-form and the Sun's wave-form all fit together — somehow.

"Not only are all of you beamed by the same galactic master program, but all of you *affect* each other. I know that nowadays none of your scientists want to believe this, but it's true. In fact, you affect the Sun as much as the Sun affects you, and down at the center of the Earth there is a spittin' image of yourself!"

"C'mon, Uncle Joe, now you're really pushing it," I spluttered, feeling as if my head were going to explode. I found myself wondering if this is how readers of *The Mayan Factor* and *Earth Ascending* must feel as they try to understand what I'm saying.

"Listen," Uncle Joe went on, clearly trying to soothe me, "I've tried my best. It's not my fault you're so one-dimensional that the facts of life sound like re-education to you. Hang in there. What I'm trying to tell you is this: the Sun is a hologram of the Earth and the Earth is a hologram of you. The cancer you humans suffer from is actually a hologram of the overabundance of humans on the Earth. At this point in time, the Earth thinks you humans are a cancer, did you know that? Put yourself into the Earth and think of humans from the Earth's point of view. What you experience as certain thoughts or premonitions or optical flickers are just your brain's way of translating a solar memory to you. Yeah, solar memory.

"That stuff all seems like a head-trip to you, I know. But when you *ride* the Zuvuya, you're hooked up with your dimensional double; your two-way communication is static-free. When it's static free, it's *ec*static! That means you've run out of static — what a blast!" Uncle Joe interrupted himself again to laugh at his own joke.

Uncle Joe got his momentum again. "You — that physical-plane slab of flesh that you call home — you act like a grounding rod for your fourth-dimensional Zuvuya keeper. If I can get fancy with you, I should say that your third-dimensional body acts like a *bio-electromagnetic* battery or grounding rod for me.

"Depending on your needs and using your 3-D self as a battery, you can send me, your dimensional double, on various kinds of missions with your consciousness and feelings. You can also stay conscious or semi-conscious or just sleep through these missions ... but you can still send me out on little interdimensional galactic errands."

"OK, great, but what's the point, Uncle Joe?"

"Listen, do you want a be a Mayan or not?" he roared back fiercely. "The point is this. Your dimensional double in its own dimension can do things you can't do here, but which can help your existence here. A little knowledge of how things *really* are can save you a heap of trouble. Unless you really do like to suffer."

"So what kind of things can the dimensional double do?" I asked, feeling confrontational.

"Like go to the center of the Earth," Uncle Joe replied breezily. "Or even to the center of the Sun. You know that stuff about the Yellow Brick Road wasn't all just fantasy." Suddenly, Uncle Joe broke into a wonderful rendition of "Somewhere Over the Rainbow." Bells tinkled inside of me. Impatience with Uncle Joe melted, and as the singing faded, so did he.

But, I realized, he had given me a lot to think about. And he's proven to be a real friend. A loyal friend. Most of all, I now know that *you* can do what he was talking about, too. In fact, that's what the program says we're supposed to do now: hook up with our dimensional doubles, our light bodies. That's what the beam I talked about in the last chapter, which ends in 25 years, is all about. By 2012 AD, like third- and fourth-dimensional outriggers, or surfers of the Zuvuya riding a wild galactic wave, we'll be able to catch up with the Maya.

Nifty, huh?

...
3
DAY
BY DAY
THE MAYAN WAY

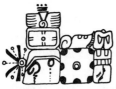 You may be thinking now that by letting Uncle Joe Zuvuya do all the talking the Maya are getting off the hook. Let's get back to the Maya, the real Maya. Let's get back to the Maya who kept what we think was such a hot calendar, the Maya who knew all about time. What is time? Did time exist before the Rolex watch? Can you tell time without a watch?

According to the Maya, the secret to time is being in synch — synchronized. Does that mean Mayans don't experience lag time? When you're out of synch, for instance, you keep missing, like a car motor in bad need of a tune up. That's not Mayan. The Mayan is his or her own best Rolex.

In fact, for starters, we could say that what makes a Mayan a real Mayan is being on time — with him or herself and with reality, clicking and ticking in time with the inner watch and with his or her dimensional double. Remember: when you're in your integrity, your double is right there, like a mirror of light or a mirror of time, flashing you your own memory circuits. Being in tune with the dimensional double is the Mayan's internal digital watch.

Now, what exactly is this *time* that a watch measures
or is in synch with? In AA — Alcoholics Anonymous —
they say "one day at a time," which is good advice. It
means "go slow, my friend, and stay in the present." We
could say that a day is how we measure time. But what
is a day?

The Earth turns once on its axis. That is a day. If you
are standing on one spot on the Earth, half of the time you
are facing towards the Sun and half of the time you are
facing away from the Sun. Both sides together make what
we call a day. The Maya call a day "kin." I like to think
of *kin* as next of kin, a relation of yours.

That's good, because the Mayan word for day, *kin*, also
means Sun. So the Sun is your kin. It is your relation. Your
brother the Sun, your father the Sun, your mother the Sun,
your sister the Sun. Whatever pleases you. It's all next of
kin. And of course, depending which planet you are on,
and in which star-system, the *kin* is always going to be
different — shorter, longer, farther, or nearer!

So you can see how the idea of a day is very relative.
Just like Uncle Joe, my double. He's my real next of kin!
As my light body daily double, Uncle Joe is also my special
agent from the Sun. I like to think of him as my kin with
the light-winning grin!

Speaking of Uncle Joe, since I started relating to him
and giving him more recognition for his role in my life,
he's started doing more and more travelling on my behalf.
Hé calls it win-win synergy, like rubbing two pieces of wood
together and getting fire. The two pieces of wood are the
third and fourth dimensions, and the fire is the synergy or the
unification and knowledge that comes from getting the two
to work together. That's the game plan — interdimensional
win-win. What this means is that the more I try to stay in
my integrity, the more light Uncle Joe gives me; the more

light he gives me, the more I flash back at him; and the more I flash back at him the more energy he gets to activate what I need to know about!

Anyway, once he really connected with me, Uncle Joe started taking off regularly and heading for what he calls the Midway Station. That's out there past the solar system *sometime* (Uncle Joe doesn't say someplace or somewhere; he says instead, *sometime*). He says this Midway Station is operated by Maya from two different star systems — Arcturus and Antares. So he calls it the Arcturus-Antares Midway Station, or the AA Midway Station for short.

Hanging out at this place, the AA Midway Station, gives Uncle Joe the view from the top. "Out here," he says, "time sure is relative! Way out here, in the Mayan Midway, it's so relative that we say, 'one Sun at a time.' We also say 'one kin at a time.'" Remember: when you are in another place in the universe, the time cycles are different — either shorter or longer — and when you are there, you are in that cycle of time.

Of course the Mayan engineering team knew (and knows) that time is all relative. You can imagine their problem: having to travel to many different star systems and planets, all with days of slightly different lengths — at least from our perspective on planet Earth. For instance, twelve years on Earth is equal to one year on Jupiter. So if you go to Jupiter for twelve years, does only one year pass? No wonder you have to be in synch with yourself in order to be a Mayan. Surfing along on their Zuvuya beams, digitalized through their light-body doubles, they zap in and out of dimensions, kinning and grinning all the way.

To do this kind of "time travelling" easily requires a ratio that is constant and at the same time flexible. What is needed is a Hunab Ku ratio: a galactic constant that allows you to put things of different proportions into the same scale; an interdimensional ratio that doesn't change but can expand or shrink to fit any size, distance — or dimension. Uncle Joe calls this ratio "the sliding Hunab Ku kazoo."

"It's a kazoo because you can blow any tune you want through it," Uncle Joe explained, "and it's sliding because it'll expand or shrink to accommodate any octave, depending on your distance from a star or the galactic source itself."

"C'mon, Uncle Joe, that's too wiggy! How can you combine octaves and distances? That's like mixing apples and oranges!"

"Well, Bud, you can look at it like this. Everything expands out like a sphere from a central source, whether that source is your planet, a star like your Sun, or the galactic core. Wherever you stand, that defines your relation to central source. If you draw a line from where you stand to central source, that would be your horizon line. So you see, from where you stand, a distance is a horizontal measurement and an octave is a vertical ratio. The closer you are to center, the shorter the kazoo and the higher the octave. The farther away you are from center, the longer the kazoo and the lower the octave. No matter how long or how short the kazoo, the octave you blow contains notes which are in the same ratio to each other. It's still an octave. Ta ta ta taa ta tat ta ta taaaaa ta taa!" Uncle Joe burst into a triumphant song, sounding for all the world as if he were blowing on a kazoo.

"Does that mean that on Uranus my octave will be 84 times lower and slower than on Earth?"

"You could say that! You see, if I can blow an octave, no matter where I am, then I can always be in synch with myself. That's how Mayans keep it together."

"That's too corny, Uncle Joe. Let's get down to brass tacks," I heard myself whining in exasperation.

"OK, so you wanna get serious. Try this then. Don't be

deceived by appearances, but become a master of illusion," Uncle Joe replied coolly.

"What do you mean by that, Uncle Joe? I thought we were talking about time; now we're into philosophy — or tricks. What is this?"

"Be patient. You're going at this the wrong way. You're thinking that time is only something you measure, like with a big yardstick, with birth at one end and death at the other. That's flat, horizontal time. You've forgotten about vertical time."

"Vertical time?" I gasped.

"Yeah. Vertical time."

"But what does vertical time have to do with illusion?" I wondered aloud, feeling totally lost.

"OK m'boy, it's like this. Everything that comes to you is an appearance of some kind, and if you're not careful, you'll get bewildered and deceived. Now why is that?" Uncle Joe scarcely paused, ready to answer his own question. "Everything you hear or see or even touch is vibration. When you're bewildered you've lost touch with your own vibration, your own frequency, and you get invaded by other vibrations. Your wave-form gets whacked. So, as any wise Mayan knows, not being deceived by appearances means staying tuned to your own vibrational frequency at all times."

"But I still don't understand what this has to do with time, Uncle Joe."

"Well, it's like this. When you're in tune with your own frequency, you become aware of what you call synchronicities or deja vus. What you've actually done is to tune your third-dimensional body into vertical time. See, Mayan time is a set of sliding frequency ranges, or octaves, that connects you *vertically* to the fourth dimension. It's like going ice fishing. On one side of the ice there is air, which can be likened to the third dimension; on the other side there is swirling cyclical water, like the fourth dimension.

"In the fourth dimension, time is radial and cyclical. It's past and future all at once. It's all over the map. It's all deja vu and synchrónicity, and does not operate like a yardstick. When you take the fishing rod of your clear consciousness and tune into the octaves of vertical time, then you experience time as all the cycles swirling through your body at once. You're resonating then, Bud. In fact, I'd say you're *transistorized*. Mayan time is transistorized time. And when you talk transistors and resonance, then you're talking numbers — the ones that describe frequency ranges and ratios — the octaves you're so fond of."

Transistorized. Uncle Joe had spoken the word with such relish. Transistorized? Wow! Then I could feel a transistor, like a little circuit, right in the middle of my head, transferring signals — from the fourth dimension? Something began to click in me. The image of a vibrating spherical holographic checkerboard, expanding in every direction and spiralling down a long tube, flickered through my *transistorized* mind.

"I get it, Uncle Joe. Once you're transistorized, *you are* the galactic constant. Or I am. Or any being is. And as long as that being is in his or her wave-form, it doesn't matter where you are — Jupiter, Uranus, or for that matter the galactic core! You're hooked up, right Uncle Joe?" For a change, I felt triumphant in my dealings with my invisible mentor.

"Right on, Buddy," Uncle Joe was cracking up, making sure I didn't think I was too smart. "In fact, I'd go even fárther. I'd say that each one of you humans is a galactic constant walkie-talkie. The joke of it is you're hooked up all the time through your brain waves to the Earth waves and the solar waves and the galactic waves. The whole show. But most of you don't realize that all you've got to do is cut a hole in the ice and fish interdimensionally!"

"And we don't realize this, or cut our hole in the ice," I interrupted, "because we're deceived by appearances."

"You bet! You got it!" Uncle Joe exclaimed.

"So does that mean that the Mayan 'calendar' is an index that matches our third-dimensional frequency ranges with fourth-dimensional frequencies? If that's the case, then if you're hooked up or transistorized, it must not matter where you are because the galactic frequency ratios are constant no matter what distance you are from the galactic core, right?"

"You're gettin' so smart, you might hardly need me any more, m'boy," Uncle Joe chuckled. "And since everything is of, by, for, and from the galaxy — heh heh — there's nothing that doesn't match up to the interdimensional galactic frequency ratios — no matter where you are. So, you're right, the point of it is — it really doesn't matter where you are."

I sat for a moment, feeling very light. Then I remembered that Uncle Joe had said something else. "But Uncle Joe, you said, 'don't be deceived by appearances, but become a master of illusion.' What about this 'master of illusion' business. How does that fit into all of this?"

"That's why I brought out the kazoo, you dummy! To be a master of illusion means tuning into vertical time and channeling the harmonics of the present moment."

"Harmonics?" I asked.

"Yeah. Harmonics. All the frequency ranges of vertical time, remember, are *octaves*. You can literally recreate fourth-dimensional time by playing those frequency ranges. You can do this by using colors to create a painting or," he giggled, "by blowin' on a kazoo! And when you go rooty toot toot, you're mastering the vibrational world of appearances. Through your playing, you're harmonizing the world of appearances to the fourth dimension. And remember, every octave has its overtones. So in the third dimension, fourth-

dimensional time is recreated or brought into being through
the overtones of music, light, and color. Sound has its
octaves and so do sight and even smell. Whoopee! You've
become a master of illusion! You're in the spotlight now,
Bud! It's show time!"

With a couple of wild and eerie ultrasonic blasts on his
kazoo, Uncle Joe was gone. As I thought about this encounter
I realized that it explained a whole lot, not only about why
the Maya had been such good artists *and* mathematicians,
but much more — more than my mind could handle.

So the Mayan calendar, the 260-unit scale called the
Tzolkin, is actually an *interdimensional* galactic constant.
It matches an Earth day — *kin* — with an interdimensional
constant — *kin*. By being in tune with ourselves, or transistorized, we match our frequencies with the interdimensional
constant. The scale of this constant can expand or shrink
to fit the size of any wave pattern — from a brain wave
to a gravity wave. And wave patterns include just about
everything, because there isn't anything that doesn't vibrate,
and if it vibrates, then it waves. Remember: even you are a
wave-form. As the Galactic Scouts say, "If it doesn't wave,
it's not real!"

The Tzolkin, this perpetual 260-day sacred calendar
used by all the ancient Mexicans, is just one application of
the interdimensional galactic constant. The calendar actually
synchronizes a 24-hour cycle day, or kin, with the whole
cyclical gamut — 13 tones strung on a lattice of 20 frequency
range possibilities. That allows for a total of 260 tonal
frequency ranges in all dimensions. Therefore by tracking one
day you can read all days, and, for that matter, all time.
This is the secret of the Day Keepers, the *Ah Kin*, those who
still keep the count and who know how to pull the sacred
cord that brings the dimensions into phase with each other.

I've been tracking the calendar, and it's true. To locate a

day is to know the whole grid, the matrix, the wave-constant of the galactic interdimensional beam. That is why the Day Keepers are seers and diviners. They are transitorized. By knowing the position of the day in the constant, and by using a set of crystals, they can channel the vibrational tone and step down the electrical charge into an image that allows them to read the time. It beats reading newspapers by a long shot!

Knowing how to extend the scale up or down, they also know that the 260-day cycle describes the 260-katun cycle of the 5125-year Great Cycle beam (a katun is a 20-year unit). You could say that every 260 days is a recap of the 260-katun Great Cycle — or vice versa. Real Mayans might feel that one day could encompass 20 years, or that 20 years on Earth is one day for them! If we add a few zeros, the 260-unit constant becomes 26,000, which is the number of years in a cycle of the precession of the signs of the zodiac. Take off the zero from 260 and what remains is 26. Aha! So is 26 the interdimensional constant?

But what is 26? 2 times 13. And what is 260? 20 times 13. While the numbers 2 or 20 are capable of doubling or increasing things, 13 is the significant number here. 13? Isn't that unlucky? Or is that just being superstitious?

Wait a minute, though. What is this issue with 13? It is simply a prime number, divisible only by itself. So why did 13 get to be an unlucky, superstitious number? In most apartment buildings in New York City, the elevator stops at a 12th floor and at a 14th floor, but not at a 13th. Who is being superstitious here — the modern New Yorkers or the "ancient" Maya?

Could the issue be that 13 was once considered the luckiest number, or at least a very special, even cosmic number? Wasn't Christ the 13th person with his group of 12 disciples, and King Arthur the 13th person with the 12 knights of the Round Table? And there are 13 moon cycles in a year and 13 baktuns, or approximately 400-year evolutionary program cycles, in the Mayan Great Cycle. Something's going on with this 13. What is it?

"It's my middle name!" Uncle Joe's voice whistled through my central channel, interrupting my Mayan meditation on numbers with an alluring jolt.

"Your middle name, Uncle Joe?" I replied, "You mean on your birth certificate it says 'Joe 13 Zuvuya?'"

"That's right, Bud. There's not a wave-catching Mayan who doesn't have one of those magic numbers as part of his or her name. But, being a 13, I am the luckiest! Hee hee hee!" Uncle Joe's strange, kazoo-like laughter faded into another ringing in my ears, leaving me alone with my meditation.

Whatever else it may mean, 13 is the Mayan galactic prime number. It is the cosmic ratio, the interdimensional key. Period. The Mayans left this galactic prime number here on Earth as a key to their cycles, the interdimensional galactic ratio. Remember, if we can get the ratio, then we have a way to put things of varying proportion into scale.

The neat and simple concept here is that the Tzolkin, the galactic constant, is nothing more than the numbers 1 through 13 repeated in sequence 20 times. That comes to a total of 260, of course.

Laid out as a 13 by 20 checkerboard matrix, the repetition of the numbers 1 through 13 creates a pattern that is similar to a weaving: a weaving of time, a weaving of reality, a weaving of dimensions. And when we look at this matrix written in the simple Mayan bar and dot numbering system, it looks like some kind of computerized chip. I call it the Harmonic Module. By looking at it, we can pick up a resonance . . . a vibration . . . the transistorized afterimage of the beam.

This computer chip, which is thirteen columns wide and

twenty columns down, can be read either as a description
of the beam *or* of the 260-day calendar. To read it, just
start at the upper left-hand corner and read down. When
you get to the bottom of one column, you then go to the
top of the next, and so on. If the top left unit is day one of
a 260-day cycle, the bottom right corner is day 260 of the
cycle. The cycle then returns to the upper left-hand corner
and starts all over again.

This computer chip can also be read as a description of
the beam. The upper left-hand corner unit begins at 3113 BC.
Each unit down is a little less than 20 years, or a katun.
The 260th katun unit, in the lower right-hand corner, takes
us from 1992 to 2012 AD — galactic blast-off!.

The 5125-year beam, of course, is divided into 13 sub-
cycles called baktuns. Each baktun, remember, is like an
evolutionary radio program, and is equal to one of the
vertical columns. It is a little more than 394 years long.
Presently we are in the 13th cycle, called Baktun 12. And
we're roaring toward the finish line, the conclusion of a
Great Cycle of 5125 years. As we might imagine, there are
big doings coming up. Uncle Joe says, "that's when we peel
the banana. The skin is like all the stuff we've invented but
won't need anymore — and we'll be just one hot banana!"

First, let's put the peel back on and flesh out this time
picture a bit more. For the Maya, there are cycles within
cycles within cycles. If we learn how to vertically tune into
the interdimensional frequencies — the octaves and all their
overtone cycles — we get to the meaning of it all.

Ancient Mexicans, like the Aztecs, called the different
ages or big cycles of time *suns*. The current 5125-year cycle,
3113 BC-2012 AD, is actually called the Fifth Sun. That
means that this last 26,000 years or so is divided into five
suns, or five world ages, each a little less than 5200 years
long. That also means we are finishing a 26,000-year zodiacal

precessional cycle. And since a precessional cycle equals
five suns, then these five suns have great significance
to Earth.

If this is so, by 2012 obviously we're headed for the big
time — hot bananas! Galactic hook-up!

Why would the ancient Mexicans, who based their ideas
of the cosmos on the Mayan calendar, call these different
periods of time *suns*?

Is it because the solar system, the Sun and its planets,
has its day and night, too? Does the solar system turn
around its source? Does it have its *kin*, its central sun?
Does everything turn around everything else? Is that why
the Maya are masters of time? If time is the measurement
of cycles, from micro-cycles to macro-cycles, is surfing the
Zuvuya the Mayan equivalent of riding a multidimensional
surfboard, the galactic constant?

If these different ages or suns also represent different
phases of a beam or a series of beams, then perhaps the
Sun really does change every 5125 years or so. But for
what reason? Do these changes in the Sun have something
to do with changes in the planetary programs as well? Does
the Sun evolve in consciousness as the galactic center evolves,
and do we evolve as the Sun changes?

Remember, the purpose of the beam that we are passing
through, like the purpose of all galactic beams, is to affect
the timing of change. One day there are dinosaurs. The next
day they are gone. One day there are woolly mammoths
and saber tooth tigers, the next day they are gone. Where
do they go? Do they die? Or are they radically transmuted —
passed through a time warp that places them into memory
capsules in the back of our brains? Will that happen to us,
too? What *will* happen to us anyway?

What we can gather is that a change in the frequency
of the beam corresponds to a change in the nature of the

different forms of life. Uncle Joe says that there really is
survival of the fittest. But to be the fittest is to possess the
ability to be transistorized — to be hooked up vertically and
to be on the beam! "And when you're that fit," he says,
"you're so happy that you want to bring everybody along
with you!"

If Hunab Ku, the galactic center, is the source of the
energy beam, and the sun is its filter, then when the energy
beam changes its frequency, the filter changes accordingly.
Of course, we might say that this is untestable, since no
one was around in 3113 BC to observe and record it. But
will we be around in 2012 AD to see if something happens
then? Hmm. We could *try* to be around. It could be
interesting!

If we are passing through this beam, does that mean
that every day the frequency changes a little? Can it be
that there is even a micro-micro-wave difference that occurs
from day to day? We know how every day feels different,
no matter what. No two days ever really feel the same, do
they? One day we've got the blahs right from the moment
we get up in the morning. The next day it's, "Hey, I'm the
greatest!" Why is that? Yet certain things are predictable —
more or less.

Day-by-day Mayan style is a little more sophisticated
than the daily horoscope in the newspaper. If we can imagine
being in one of those squares in the 13 by 20 checkerboard,
then travelling from the upper left-hand corner to the bottom
right corner is day-by-day, Mayan style. If we can imagine
each one of these squares as a ratio of one day to one of the
nearly 20-year katun cycles, then we are placing ourselves
in relation to the beam. We are vertically hooking up, and
the interdimensional frequencies are coming through. Sure,
every day has its different quality. But we attune our wave-
form to the day. We behold the sun. We are grateful. We

know that we are a planetary program, a hologram of the Earth, and á hologram of the Sun.

Know that we are the cumulative fulfillment of a wave that has been building for over 5100 years. Everyone is a time capsule. Even though it may not be obvious or at all apparent to us, everything we are doing is in partial fulfillment of the planet receiving an evolutionary doctoral degree by 2012. "Ph.D. in planetary surfin'," Uncle Joe calls it, "awarded by the waxed galactic constant surfboard of review — all sporting their Hunab Ku suntans! Hee hee hee!"

Knowing that this is what we're going for is what Uncle Joe calls "putting the point back in your appointment book." He says, "ask yourself: why am I doing what I am doing today? Be honest. Are you working and meeting with others to benefit others and the Earth? Or is it just to benefit yourself, to make a profit, and then get out of the office as fast as you can?"

This may sound like it is asking us to be high-minded. And it is. Because from the point of view of Earth's passage through the beam, the critical moment has come. In fact Harmonic Convergence, in August, 1987, has come and gone. Do we know what's happening on the planet, or what's happening to the planet? Has anything changed?

Let's beam in Uncle Joe to give us his perspective from the AA Midway Station. This is our chance to view ourselves from out there in the galaxy.

"Hey, Uncle Joe, are you there?"

"Sure am. What do you need to know?"

"Can you fill us folks in on what's going on with the planet since Harmonic Convergence?"

There was a pause. Then, eerily blasting through a galactic echo chamber, came Uncle Joe laughing and singing, "Wipe-out!" I could hear the 1960s rhythm section riffing away.

"Wipe-out? Is it that bad, Uncle Joe?" I asked him. In my mind's eye I could see the whole of modern civilization, its rockets and freeways crazily careening across a fantastic beach that was twinkling with star patterns and spectral wave forms.

"Yeah, Bud, from where we see it, 'wipe-out' is the right word, at least for your civilization." Uncle Joe came back from rock-n-roll heaven to a more normal tone of voice.

"To tell you the truth, Bud, it's not good. Planet's sick. Oh, I know there's some moves to stop a few things like cut down on the fluorocarbons so the leak in the ozone layer won't grow so fast, and reduce nuclear missiles, but there's still too much greed. Don't know if you're gonna make it or not. What you don't understand down there is that too much damage has already been done, so some things have already been set in motion. Be a couple of years before you see the mudpies hit the fan, but when it hits, it'll hit hard. The days of your industrial civilization are numbered."

"Uncle Joe, c'mon! Is that all you have to say? That's as bad as the evening news. What about all those people who got behind Harmonic Convergence? Didn't that do anything?"

"Well. Hard to say. But you know up here we've got a saying: *when the light hits, the dark gets tough.* Harmonic Convergence was like a light going on. Ignorance can't stand it when a flashlight gets shined in its eyes. So it's like the craziness is going to be getting more crazy. The people who got some of the light, they're going kind of crazy, too. But they've got to hang in there. I bet a lot of them even question whether they should've even tried; maybe think they'd feel better the old way. But the old way's gone, run by moral sleazes who really aren't even here! Stock market's crashed. Economy's flip-floppin like a fish outta water. The Earth is a-wobblin' and a-rumblin', greenhouse effect, quakes and all that . . ."

"What can they do, Uncle Joe?"

"Make life boats fast," he giggled. "Their civilization is a sinking ship. Get together with each other and let each other know who they are and where they are. See what kind of resources they've got all together. You see, it's clean up time. Earth's getting ready to clean herself up. The people have to clean up, too. Get honest. Be truthful. Get rid of what they don't need. That means inside and out. Exert their highest intention and act on their integrity."

"But Uncle Joe, doesn't anyone up there care?"

"Oh yeah. They care a lot. You see, this is a high level project. It's got ramifications that go a long ways. No one wants to see this project get blown. In fact, there's a lot of 'em up here ready to help. But it's all in the timing, you know. You've got five years of rough weather ahead of you, at least up through 1992. But right now you can begin to prepare. Help can be available in five years *if* you want it. But you've all gotta prepare."

"That sounds pretty ominous, Uncle Joe. I thought getting into this interdimensional stuff was supposed to be fun," I responded, becoming more and more dismayed.

"It's fun all right. But you're all still too third-dimensional, and you're paying the consequences for constructing something grandiose from too narrow a perspective. If you get what I mean. You see, it's not at all like you think it is."

"What do you mean, it's not at all like we think it is?"

"Well, first of all, this Earth of yours. You don't own it. If anything, it owns you. And it's alive. It's a living intelligent being. Oh, you're part of it all right. You're like one of its skins, or actually, you're like its receiver skin, its atmospheric radar system. All of you human beings are like a giant nervous radar web that processes information at a pretty

high level. It could be a lot greater if you woke up to what
it's really all about.

"Right now you just process stuff you think will reinforce
your little ambitions, and you bombard each other with it
through your electronic nervous system. That's your radio
and television networks. But what gibberish! Tsk! Tsk!"

"Uncle Joe! Aren't you coming on a little snobbish?" I
asked, "I mean, now you're sounding like a yuppie."

"If I'm snobbish or a yuppie," he answered slightly in a
huff, "it's only thanks to you, Bud. Since you started paying
attention to me, I've gotten the credits to be able to get up
to the AA Midway Station a little more often than I used
to. And I like it up there. It's a lot less confusing. The air
is rarified, fourth-dimensional beings are a little more evolved.
And up there, I'm able to reach for dimensions beyond the
fourth. I can see better up there."

"Ok. So put it back on me, Uncle Joe. I guess this is
the price of my own education. Just don't get snobbish
with me personally."

"Depends. Just don't get chicken with your integrity,
and keep your wave-form clean. That's not asking too much.
Is there anything more you need to know? The gang here is
playing Arcturian chess, and we're using human holograms.
I'd like to get back to it."

"You're doing *that* kind of thing while we're down here
in the eye of the storm? C'mon Uncle Joe. Give me a break."

"I'd love to give you a break. But don't judge what I'm
doing by your standards. Do you know what Arcturian
chess is all about?"

"You're right. I don't know. What *is* Arcturian chess
all about?"

"Arcturian chess is played only when we got a planetary
situation like you've got down there now. The live holograms
we're playing with are the holograms we observed of the

people participating in Harmonic Convergence. You know, the famous 144,000. The Pleiadian team has joined us, so we're cookin'. The object of the game is to get these holograms into the center of the Earth no later than 1993, your time. If we move them down into the center of the Earth, then Earth's got an intelligent human-light grid operating with the intelligence grid of the Earth, down there in the crystal core."

"Wait a minute, Uncle Joe." Something in me resisted his words. "Are you manipulating our holograms; moving us against our will?"

"C'mon Bud, like I said, it's not at all like you think it is. Every moment of the day you're pushing up against an infinite number of possibilities. In fact, each of these possibilities lives in its own parallel universe. Have you got any idea how many parallel universes there are? So relax. Where we are, at the AA Midway, we've got the best view, so we're just pushing for the best parallel universe possible. But it's up to you to choose it!"

"Uncle Joe, I get it. That's wild! I should let you go. Thanks!"

"One other thing. This day-by-day stuff you've been talking about. It's not bad. In fact it really means a lot right now. You might let your friends know that day-by-day they should take a minute and just tune into the Earth. In fact, they could even tune into the center of the Earth.

"What you do is send an imaginary beam down there to where this hologram is taking form, and let Earth know you care. You can then take one of the Earth's energy beams back from the core to the surface, wherever you are. When you get experienced at that and are able to send your dimensional double down there, then we call that *Earth diving*. It may sound corny. But like I said, the way you've done things down there, you don't know the half of it. And until you all get that vertical time together, and go interdimensional fishing, you won't know the whole of it, that's for sure."

Uncle Joe trailed off into laughter. Then he was gone again.

Uncle Joe was really getting out there. I noticed that he was getting more wrathful — and wiggy. What the hell, though. He's right. The more I pay attention to him and engage him, the more powerful he gets, and the more I feel and know. That's not a bad trade-off, is it?

 "Hey, José! You there! Give me your attention!" Uncle Joe paused. "By the way, you don't mind if I call you 'José' from time to time, do you Bud?"

"Oh, Uncle Joe. It's you again," I replied. "Of course I don't mind if you call me José. But I've been meaning to ask you, is there a reason why you call me 'Bud'?"

"'Course there is," Uncle Joe chuckled, "You're a budding Earthling, an Earth Bud, Bud. Get with the program. Harmonize that hologram of yours," Uncle Joe broke off into laughter once again.

No doubt about it. Uncle Joe was getting more familiar with me, and very persistent, showing up frequently at unexpected moments. He had canned his act of just coming to me in my siestas. I never knew when he'd show up. I could tell things were getting serious.

"So listen, José. I got a confession to make."

"What's that?" I asked, somehow smelling a rat. But ... maybe he was being sincere this time.

"I dumped on you, kid. I got carried away with being allowed to play Arcturian chess. It went to my head. I owe you an apology . . . and a whole lot of explanations."

"Really?" This was a new move on his part. Maybe time on the AA Midway Station was keeping him humble after all. "What sort of explanations?" I asked, genuinely intrigued.

"About what's going on. You know, you asked me about what was happening with the planet, and I gave you a rush of information. It wasn't fair. It was too much. I want to go more slowly this time. But I have to tell you a story."

"A story? What kind of story?"

"Well, it's a story about Atlantis."

"Atlantis?" I asked. "What's Atlantis got to do with the Mayans?" I was unsure now. Was Uncle Joe going to sideswipe me with some strange, lurid, occult tales?

"Don't worry, José. This isn't some New Age trip. And the Mayans have a lot to do with it. It's like this. You found out that the Maya weren't just an ancient people. Sure, there's Mayans a-plenty in the Yucatan living just like they lived two thousand years ago, just biding their time, planting corn, waiting for the cycle to blow over, waiting for us to catch up with them. Right?

"But you also know that the Mayans had something to do with Harmonic Convergence, just because their calendar is hooked up interdimensionally to Grand Central — Hunab Ku — in a way that no other human calendar is. You yourself called that connection the Mayan Factor, because it's all in the timing, and the Mayans, well they invented time, right?"

"How can I argue against myself, Uncle Joe? Go on," I replied, feeling sucked in by his sly build-up.

"And you also know that the Maya came here originally with some kind of purpose and mission, because things here weren't quite together with the human DNA. They came to show that it's possible to live in harmony with nature, and they came to leave their calling card — what you call the galactic constant — that 260-unit 'harmonic module.'

"Isn't there something about this planet that gives you that haunted feeling? Like 'Paradise Lost' but not yet 'Paradise Regained'? Well, when the Maya came here, the ones you write about in your book, anyway, it was already 'Paradise Lost', wasn't it? So the Mayans' part in this little cosmic drama is 'ET came and ET went.' What do you think about that story, 'Paradise Lost'?"

Uncle Joe was right. A strange haunting came over me. I began to get a sense of the *largeness* of the galactic drama. Troops of memories crashed into my head as if they were being blasted through a dammed-up Zuvuya circuit. I could see Christ in Gethsemane, Lucifer with his rebellious angels, worlds and star-systems hurtling through space, geometric patterns and cellular structures joined together, glimpses of wild, exotic, crystal pyramid cities rising up out of deserts and ocean floors, exploding into billowing orange and violet clouds on countless planets throughout the universe. Bam! Blam! What was going on?

"Hee Hee Hee," Uncle Joe was laughing, though it sounded more like he was wheezing through his kazoo, looking for some "Twilight Zone" cough drops.

"OK. You got the picture," he continued. "There is *something* to that Lucifer story. Cosmic fifth-dimensional organization man carried away by his free will imposes his higher dimensional will prematurely on the genetic mudpies of certain planets. He gets a few others in the neighborhood to join him. They get caught in a galactic sting operation. What to do? The top-dimensional upper-ups quarantine him — and the 37 planets involved — and announce: 'No interference on these planets until the genetic material ripens to understand the real meaning of responsibility and free will.'

"In the meantime, because the genetic mudpies have

been messed with by Lucifer, the beings, let's call them humanoids, develop with slightly messed-up circuits. It's called premature free will. It makes for illusions about reality and power trips over others. But once the timing was interfered with, there's nothing to be done until they get to the point of seeing their own mistakes. Sound familiar?"

Puzzle pieces began to fall into place. "So this is the kind of stuff they talk about up on the AA Midway Station, Uncle Joe?"

"Yeah, Bud. It's like a galactic AA meeting. People — well I guess you could call them 'people' — come together and share their stories about where and when they got tempted by free will, how they abused it, what they learned from it, and what they're doing to make amends."

"That's neat, Uncle Joe, but let's get back to Atlantis. You started off by saying you were going to tell the story about Atlantis, and now here we are with Lucifer."

"Well, I had to tell you this part first, because it's like the background, the scenery for the Atlantis story, but now I'll get into it, the 'True History of Atlantis.' Actually, there's lots of Atlantises — and Lemurias, too. Projects started in Lucifer's free-will zone. Look at a map of Mars and you'll see they've got an Atlantis and Lemuria there, too. Pretty strange, huh? There's a face of an ancient humanoid on Mars near some pyramids. Even what seems like a megalithic stone circle. And then out there past Mars, there's the asteroid belt. That was a planet once: Maldek, some call it. What do you s'pose happened to it?"

Uncle Joe's words faded out for a moment. The haunted feeling intensified. Is everything that is now happening on our planet somehow a *repeat*, yet another take in a galactic recording studio by a band that couldn't quite get its chord changes down? Sensing my melancholy, Uncle Joe picked up the story again.

"But, back to *our* Atlantis. First of all the *time*. With your Mayan ratio, the galactic constant, you know that we've got these cycles that are close to 26,000 years long, and you already know how everything fits into everything else. That's the harmonic module. Everything turns around inside everything else. The 'bigger' turns around in the 'even bigger' and the 'even bigger' turns around inside the 'bigger yet' and so on. But you never really get to the end of it: the cosmic hologram!

"Anyway, the next cycle up from the 26,000-year cycle is the 104,000-year cycle, which is four 26,000-year cycles. That's a long time ago, or, as they say up on the AA Midway, there's a lotta spin to that one! Well, sometime just beyond that 104,000-year spin, in another part of the galaxy, there was a planet, and that planet was called . . . Atlantis."

Something about the way Uncle Joe pronounced "Atlantis" made it sound poetic, soft, and alluring. I felt more memories being jogged — dislodged from some subterranean shelf at the back of my brain.

"Yeah, Atlantis," Uncle Joe went on. "This planet, well, it was pretty evolved. Things were moving in the right direction, and they were getting the picture pretty clear. But one day it became evident that a cosmic catastrophe was approaching them. That's the kind of thing that occurs to test us, to give us another challenge. It always happens when everything is just super, then, bang! You get hit on the head, and someone says, 'hey dummy, did you think you had gotten to the top already?' Well, that's just what happened to Atlantis. No fault of their own really. Just a test.

"Now, before they lowered the boom on this poor doomed planet, a council was called way upstairs, and from this council, 12 were sent down to Atlantis. What to do . . . what to do . . . The elders of Atlantis met with the 12 council elders from on high. The concern was to salvage the evolutionary achievement which Atlantis had already attained."

"What do you mean by 'evolutionary achievement already attained,' Uncle Joe?" I interrupted.

"It's like this. Those Atlanteans had worked real hard, and collectively they were getting close to major graduation. Anyway, you'll get it. Just listen.

"So they had to come up with a plan. It wasn't easy. There was a core of 144,000 Atlanteans. They divided this core into 12 groups. And each of those 12 groups divided into another 12 groups, on down till you got 12,000 subgroups. Your Mayan 13 is there, because at the center of each group of 12 was an invisible 13th: the interdimensional vertical time link. You might call it the spiritual sum of the 12 put together. So anyway, all these groups formed like a network.

"The next step was where to go and what to do. It was decided to migrate to another planet. Since this was a kind of experiment, they had to find a planet in the experimental zone of the galaxy."

"The experimental zone? Geez, Uncle Joe, what kind of universe is this?"

"Yeah, José. The experimental zone. That's Lucifer's turf. Anyway, the planet they wanted to go to was located in a star system which actually forms a part of the Pleiades system. Did you know that? Did you know that the 26,000-year cycles have to do with the fact that your sun rotates around the Pleiades every 26,000 years? And every 104,000 years it goes around four times. That's a super solar year."

"Huh?" More memory pieces were jogging around in the back of my head. Why was all this starting to sound strangely familiar?

"Yeah, Bud, that's an important piece. See, the Central Sun for *this* part of the galaxy is located in what you call the Pleiades. The name of that sun is Alcyone. The next

star over from Alcyone is Maya. You connecting the
dots there?"

I was. No doubt about it. Lights were going on all over
my head.

"Of course, for the Atlanteans to come to what's actually
the seventh star of the system centered around Alcyone, the
whole thing had to be checked out with the keeper of the
central star, the grand Pleiadean wizard, the 'ancient of
days,' Layf-Tet-Tzun. He's your great uncle, you know.

"My great uncle? How's that?"

"Well, you know how I'm your fourth-dimensional
double, and we're part of this system called Earth going
around the Sun, which the Maya call Ahau Kin. And,
remember because of that we're all next of kin. The Day
Keepers are the Ah Kin, and our star, Ahau Kin, is obviously
related to the Central Sun, Alcyone. Ahau Kin is the seventh
star going around Alcyone. The keeper of our star is Ahau
Kinich. Naturally Ahau Kinich is real close with Layf-
Tet-Tzun."

"But who are these people — Ahau Kinich and Layf-
Tet-Tzun?"

"They're fifth-dimensional lighties, Bud. Just as I'm your
uncle, they're your great uncles. But the really real great
uncle, that's Layf-Tet-Tzun."

"But are they guys?"

"Only because you're a guy. If you were a woman,
they'd be ladies to you. But really they're both sexes, and
more. Let's not lose track of the story. Once Layf-Tet-Tzun
got filled in on the scoop about Atlantis, and thought about
it, he gave his reply:

" 'With this advance group of Atlanteans, I can advance
my own graduation. I could be ready to graduate in 104,000
of those Earth-years. Those 144,000 who were preparing to
graduate can do time on the Earth planet, but they'll have

to wait through four cycles, and when the time comes, 104,000 years down the star-track, they can be my replacement. The Atlanteans can help out that planet — eventually, but not yet. They have to wait 78,000 years before they can think of mingling. Even then they'll have to be careful. That's a dangerous zone that planet's in. The Atlanteans could get in over their heads.' "

As Uncle Joe retold old Layf-Tet-Tzun's words, I could almost see this keeper of the Central Sun, an androgynous wizard, solitary through what must have seemed like an eternity within the fiery dimensional chambers of that distant star, Alcyone.

"Once they knew where to go," Uncle Joe continued, "the 144,000 Atlanteans formed into their light networks. Just before the catastrophe rolled over the planet, Atlantis, burning it till it wasn't even a cinder in space, the inter-dimensional migration took off. Whoooosh!

"Now down here, there wasn't just one Atlantis. There were three phases. Each of these three ran through a cycle of 26,000 years. The first ran from 104,000 to 78,000 years ago. The second from 78,000 to 52,000 years ago, and the third from 52,000 to 26,000 years ago. Of course, the Atlanteans were under strict orders not to mingle or inter-breed with the other folks. And they didn't. They wouldn't want to anyway. You know how it was 104,000 years ago, don't you? Just humanoid types back then. Quest for fire was about as far as they'd gone.

"Anyhow, the first two Atlantises were destroyed by natural cyclic events. You know, when one of those 26,000-year cycles closes out, something major always happens. Some kind of elemental convulsion. Maybe a flood, or, if the Earth is kind, just an ice age. You're still young, Bud. You got something to look forward to in 2012. Yep. You sure do."

"You mean like the Earth shifting its axis — a pole shift?"

"Could be. Or maybe could be another ice age. Sure looks like that now. Or maybe a combination. Who knows?

"Anyway, these kinds of things weren't too much of a bother to the Atlanteans. After all, they'd already come over from another planet. But then when we get the third Atlantis, the last before this one . . ."

"You mean, Uncle Joe, we're Atlantis, too?"

"No, Atlantis *four,*" Uncle Joe chuckled over his pun. "But you're right. This thing you're living through, it's the last Atlantis, the fourth one. There's major amnesia about it. So we just keep on creating it, unconsciously though. And that's the problem: unconscious, no memory. That's why we've got these AA Groups now — Atlantean Amnesiacs. Get it, Bud? It's true. That is what's really behind AA: Atlantean Amnesiacs! People hiding out, boozing and drugging, denying memories, because there's no safe place to remember. But after this fourth one, there can't be any more Atlantises, at least not on this planet. The options have been used up. That's a big point to remember, Bud.

"But, back to our story. This third Atlantis, it was underwater. Big crystal domes under what you call the Atlantic Ocean. That's the stuff with the Bermuda Triangle. That's the remnants of the third Atlantis' interdimensional zone. Underwater they had good communication with the dolphins. Those dolphins you know, they originally came from the Sirius star system. Isn't that far out?"

"You bet, Uncle Joe," I replied. Images of vibrational dolphins streaming through interstellar space, surfing on a Mayan interdimensional beam, splashed through my mind. "You're really stretching me out."

"Goes with the territory, Bud. You wanted to play interdimensionally, so now I'm giving it to you.

"As for the Atlanteans, though, this time around they

got themselves into some deep trouble. They started to live in disregard of cosmic law. Fooling around with the laws of nature. That's called disconnecting knowledge and wisdom. And even worse, they got into power games. Some people got fooled into giving their power away. And, of course, other people were there to take that power. And when that started to happen, they got into the worst. People imposing their will over others. That's the big cosmic no-no, the control game. Well, that was the end. That spelled doom. Will over nature and will over others. That'll do it every time. Sound familiar, Bud?"

"Sure does, Uncle Joe," I had to agree. "That's what we're doing down here, day in and day out in every way we can, from the cradle to the grave."

"Yep. Real familiar. So by this time, the 144,000 had forgotten their mission. Things were bad. The last king of Atlantis was a man named Markus Morpheus. During his reign they used drugs to keep people disempowered. And they had these crystal devices, like walkman head-sets, that they also used to keep people under control. *Control*. That's the biggie. Control. You ever notice how that's the button, the control button, that really keeps things seething? Nobody wants to give up control."

As I pondered Uncle Joe's question, an uneasiness overcame me. My solar plexus got that tight feeling. My button was pushed. I felt it — the struggle to maintain control ... control over what? And for what reason? Protection and control and defense and punishment. All these things merged into the dark web of driven confusion called modern life.

"So the third Atlantis blew," Uncle Joe picked up the thread of his story. "And it blew big. Cataclysm. Bad scene to the max. All the crystal bubbles shattered. The oceans heaved. The land shook. It sank to the bottom of the sea. That was Plato's Atlantis — gone!"

What a story. It was giving me the shivers.

"It's sinking in, huh Bud?" Uncle Joe chuckled, appreciative of his own punning. "Now at the time this happened, the Earth was naturally shifting to its next evolutionary phase. An ice age was spreading. And, finally, the humanoids were tooled up for their big evolutionary hour. *Homo sapiens* you'd call 'em. They emerged at precisely this time. They were close to equal in potential to the Atlanteans. And since the Atlanteans had created havoc on our planet, as karmic recompense the Earth now had them incarnate — be born among the *Homo sapiens*. That was their karma. Couldn't be pure Atlanteans anymore.

"But these *Homo sapiens* were already developing under a handicap. Remember Lucifer? The humans already had their genetic wiring just a little messed up, suffering from tendencies to premature free-will.

"So here we are in Paradise Lost. And the Atlanteans are now mingled in among us. And it's the last ice age. What a scene! But it wasn't that bad. The leaders figured out a really clever thing to do. You see, people back then had little material technology. And with the ice age, little chance for it either. But they were still pretty well hooked up to their dream bodies, their fourth-dimensional doubles. So what they decided to do was to dream the collective dream. They knew the ice age wouldn't last forever, so if they dreamed their collective dream, they could dream what it was they had to do after the ice age. They could dream their tools and their tasks. They could dream everything that was to come. Clever huh? That's *Homo sapiens* for you.

"So that's what they did. They entered the dreamtime, together, collectively. They put their ESP to good use. All around the planet, little tribes, little ice age clans, sleeping together, their heads to the fire, dreaming the same dream. A network of dreamers. And because there were the Atlanteans

among them, over the years, the centuries, the millenia,
they slowly created a collective *dreamtime* Atlantis. It was
the Atlantis of before. And it was the Atlantis of what was
to come. And like the Atlantis of before, the third Atlantis,
this dreamtime Atlantis blew apart.

"It was a real trauma. Everyone had the same nightmare.
They woke up startled and confused. No one could quite
remember what had happened. When this occurred, the ice
age was about over. That was about 12-13,000 years ago. The
mammoths were gone. The Earth was warm. And people
had to pick up the pieces, the fragments of the dream, and
try to set out to do what they had dreamed they would do."

Uncle Joe Zuvuya paused. I got a ringing in my ears
and I could feel the sadness of that time. It was awesome.

"Slowly," Uncle Joe continued his narration, "the people
got it together as best they could. Something in the dream
they remembered had told them about seeds and planting.
So they started to find seeds and plant them. Something
else they remembered told them about baskets and weaving
and clay. So they started figuring that out, too. It wasn't
too bad. And sometimes some of the symbols would come
back to various ones of them. The symbols — that was like
the cosmic language, the language of the cosmic laws. And
so a little of that came back, too. And they tried to live the
best they could.

"Now here's the part where your Maya come in again.
You can see how the Maya might be Layf-Tet-Tzun's scouting
party. Of course, Layf-Tet-Tzun was pretty anxious about all
of this. He had been looking forward to graduation in 26,000
years, and now it was like a setback. The 144,000 had
gotten themselves into a heck of a spot, mingled in with a
group that had scarcely begun to dream about civilization —
and they'd been through it a number of times already. In
fact the Atlanteans had been ready to do it one last time

before they had their graduation.

"Sometime about the end of the third Atlantis, the Maya had been sent to do a surveillance. Could the project be salvaged? That was Layf-Tet-Tzun's request of the Maya: to figure out whether or not Project Earth was an evolutionary write-off. Layf-Tet-Tzun didn't need the tax break. He needed the graduation.

"So the Maya came down and checked out the scene. Some teams kept up surveillance for a few thousand years. This is what they reported back to Layf-Tet-Tzun. Listen carefully, José. I got this directly from an Antarean in a hologram swap:

THE MAYAN REPORT

" 'Chances of salvage, fair. Conditions good, however. At .80 of the current 26,000-year beam there will be an amping-up of frequency. That'll correspond to the initiation of the free-form civilization sweepstakes run. This is to be matched by a 5125-year acceleration phase beam that will not hit synchronization until minus 25 years from beam completion. Very high risk since that leaves only 25 years for Atlantean memory course correction. Also, humans won't be in a position to invite assistance until that point: minus 25 years from beam phase exit.

" 'Recommendation: Mayan intervention during last .20 of the 26,000-year beam to correct for errors in planetary beam synchronization. Maximum beam phase for synchronic engineering: Baktun 9, subcycle 10.

" 'Request: Permission to initiate two-part intervention procedures immediately. Agent 13 66 56, Pacal Votan, available for all pre- and post-intervention surveillances, as well as for tour of duty at maximum second phase-intervention.

" 'Residuals: Will leave a genetic type — Mayan — on planet. Will also leave behind art treasures and the galactic code, but with well-concealed instructions.' "

What a report! Uncle Joe delivered it like a well-primed computer.

"Of course," said Uncle Joe, returning to his normal voice, "old Layf-Tet-Tzun, he granted the Mayan engineering team its request. What else could he do, Bud? He was impatient. He wants to graduate. The Mayan engineering team is trustworthy. No one's got a better map and more smarts than those Mayans when it comes to getting around inter-dimensionally. And no one can beat them at planetary intervention games. They camouflage themselves so well that hardly anyone can figure out that they're ETs. Pretty sharp, huh, Bud?"

I was breathless. Was this the inside scoop? What a shot!

"Well, the rest is history," Uncle Joe laughed. But he was right. The rest *is* history. At least until now, and maybe now the history is over.

"So tell me, Uncle Joe, do you mean that Harmonic Convergence was like a signal planted in the Earth that would go off at just that moment in time?"

"Something like that, as far as I can tell. It was a signal cued to the genetic program, or the planetary program, whichever you want. It's on the beam, anyway you look at it."

"So what happens now? Where are the Atlanteans? How do we get our memory back? Do the Atlanteans still remember that they're the Atlanteans? Are the Maya coming back? Are they behind the UFOs?" The questions burst out of me nonstop. My mind was a welter of images, of underwater cities slowly swept and reshaped by deep tidal sands, and of metallic discs, UFOs, buzzing and sweeping the planet's amnesia-wracked hologram . . .

"No way, José! Chill out. Back to your wave-form. All I can tell you right now is you've probably got an Atlantean somewhere in your neighborhood. What we gotta do now is figure out a way for all of 'em to remember who they are, and get back into their networks, so they figure out what they have to do next!"

"And the rest of the humans, Uncle Joe, what happens to them?"

"Don't worry. This is their big chance. In evolution comes a time when all advance together or none advance at all.

"But, listen José, I gotta go back to the AA Midway Station. We got another 12-step, 12-person meeting tonight. It's supposed to be hot and I don't want to miss it. So like I keep telling you, get with the program — that's where it's at."

5
THE
CAMPAIGN
FOR THE EARTH

As I began to understand it, Harmonic Convergence was not just a one-shot deal. It was a well-timed Earth signal. The Earth is now shifting, adjusting to the wave motion, and preparing herself for her next evolutionary jump. Twenty-five years is not a very long time, especially compared to the 5100-year phase of the beam that preceded Harmonic Convergence. So from the Earth's point of view, what's the scoop?

I have been trying to get Uncle Joe to give me some answers. It's not easy. He has been enjoying those AA meetings out there at the Midway Station so much that he has become an AA junkie. That's not all bad either. There is a lot of moral uplift to those meetings, and obviously a lot of information. But things are critical down here.

So I decided to try and get Uncle Joe to do some exercise. Anyone would need exercise after sitting around like Uncle Joe at all those AA meetings, so between meetings I thought I should send him Earth diving. Remember, we talked about that a couple of chapters ago. It involved setting up a matrix or a grid at the core of the Earth — the crystal core, Uncle Joe called it.

And I had questions, too — questions that needed answering if I was to go on. Like, what was the relation between Earth diving and Atlantis? And what was the connection between the 144,000 of Harmonic Convergence and the 144,000 of Atlantis? I needed some explanations.

From my point of view, or anyone's third-dimensional point of view for that matter, we don't see much. We are not vertically hooked up, so all we see is the parking lot and the lines at the airport and the delays in the airplanes and the freeway traffic. And the only answers we get are like those prerecorded messages we receive when we make a call. But what does it look like from the Earth's point of view? It seemed that sending Uncle Joe Earth diving was certainly one way of getting some answers.

"Uncle Joe, come on through, we've got work to do," I called out to him — or *in* to him. Who knows where that fourth dimension is?

Intensifying my concentration, I waited. There was a pause, and then the sound of wind, but very high-pitched and almost piercing. Then came a sputtering, like somebody was choking on a chicken bone and playing the kazoo at the same time.

"Whew!" I finally heard Uncle Joe's voice. "It sure is dense down here. And those vapors, gadzooks! Things must be slow going, huh, Bud?"

"You said it," I replied. "It's like there's no direction. Everything is whacky. It's a little like one of those department store displays where all the TV sets are on but no one is watching and all the stereos are on but no one is listening. You can't even find a floor manager to answer questions."

"You got something on your mind, José. What is it?"

"You got me there, Uncle Joe," I answered, relieved that I had been psyched out and could get on with what was on my mind. "Yeah, I do have something on my mind. A couple of things actually."

"Oh yeah? And what might they be?"

"Well, one thing that's been bothering me is the 144,000. There are 144,000 from Atlantis, and there are 144,000 from Harmonic Convergence. What is that about? Is it all part of the Mayan plot? Is there some elite group forming here? And what does that have to do with Earth diving?" I blurted the whole thing out.

"Aha! Squirming are you?"

"Well, if you want to look at it that way, Uncle Joe," I replied. No doubt about it, I was feeling uncomfortable, defensive. But I persisted. "Listen. If there are 144,000 people, are they special? Who are they? And what about everybody else? Are they left out? Where's the justice?"

"Simmer down, Bud. Let me ask you a question. Wouldn't it be arrogant of someone to presume he or she was one of the elect 144,000? I mean, would you go around *proclaiming* that you were one of the 144,000?"

"No way, Uncle Joe. We have enough ego trips going on down here as it is. What gives then? How does it work?"

"OK, Bud. Here's the scoop. You're right. No way would it work if everybody was saying he or she was one of the special programs. It's OK to think you *might* be one of 'em. But you don't know. That's the evolutionary safeguard.

"More to the point, everybody's gotta think they *might* be one of 'em. That way everybody's pulling for everybody else. And besides, with all the different generations of inter-breeding since Atlantis, everyone's gotta be holding some memory of it, some piece of the puzzle."

"So it's like we have an Atlantean memory democracy, huh, Uncle Joe?"

"Yeah, Bud, now you're cookin'."

"So what do we do then? It's a mess down here. Like you said, it's really dense. We have to get things moving."

"OK. Now, no one really knows who the 144,000 are.
Fact is, because of the interbreeding, it's not like 144,000
people so much as it is 144,000 types or styles of experience
that everybody passes through. So it's like everybody has
to wake up through remembering what they have experienced,
and who and where they have been. Got that, José?"

"All right, Uncle Joe! That means we really are multidimensional in so many ways that it makes me dizzy."

"Better you're dizzy thinking about it than so numbed-
out you'd think I was crazy talking about it, hee hee hee!"
Regaining his composure, Uncle Joe continued. "It's OK,
Bud. Let's just get on with it. In this kind of situation you
do the best you can. You hang out with the question mark;
that way' the answers will come to you. At this point in
time, if you think you've got the answer, you're dead wrong.
So what do you do? You assume the best. Go Atlantean!
Start forming into small groups. If you can get a group
going for yourself once a week, then you're on your way.
Eventually, if your group gets up to 12, then you're really
doing the Atlantean memory course correction."

"That makes sense, but what's in it for you, Uncle Joe?"

"Good question, Bud. What's in it for me — and all the
other dimensional doubles — is this: remember, you're my
real estate investment. All of you third-dimensional humans
are the real estate investment of the Dimensional Doubles
Progressive Field Association."

"The *what*? What are you talking about, Uncle Joe? This
sounds like some capitalist exploitation trip. Here we've
established an Atlantean memory democracy, and now you
come along with your Dimensional Doubles Progressive
Field Association. What's going on?" I was exasperated.

"Relax, Bud. This is all part of interdimensional play.
Do you wanna have fun or not?"

I recognized I had lost my cool. Did I really think Uncle

Joe had a mean wave in his interdimensional form? Contritely, I asked, "What is the Dimensional Doubles Progressive Field Association?"

"It's something that developed out of our AA meetings on the Midway Station. You see, there's been a number of us from Earth up there. Higher Power graduates we're called. But it's still another meeting to us.

"Anyway, we got to talking one day about our shortcomings and how to make amends. We all realized we had kind of fallen alseep on the job, too. Because of that, we saw that our investments had gotten bad tenants. We hadn't been paying attention. All sorts of stinky ego-trips had begun to occupy our real estate. We couldn't blame the real estate, really, for all of it. We had to take our half of the responsibility.

"So what we figured out was that we should form into a collective: The Dimensional Doubles Progressive Field Association! Our intention is to improve our property — you third-dimensional human wave-forms — so that we get greater returns. But in order for this to work, it's got to work both ways. You see, if we just pour energy into you without telling you what we want, it won't do you any good. You'd get crazy ideas that would make you think you really *knew* that you're one of the 144,000. Nope, gotta work both ways. You gotta match your energy and your field with ours."

"Well, how do we do that, Uncle Joe?"

Simple. You form into the Crystal Earth Energy Network Home Improvement Association. Even though you're just leasing that body, you still have to have pride of ownership and . . ."

I had to interrupt Uncle Joe. "Come on, first we get the Dimensional Doubles Progressive Field Association, and now the . . . what?"

"The Crystal Earth Energy Network Home Improvement Association," Uncle Joe asserted triumphantly. "That's the collective *you* form to match the energy of our collective. It's not hard to do. You start with your groups of 12. Each one of 'em is like a neighborhood chapter of the Crystal Earth Energy Network Home Improvement Association. It's also a fine example of the Atlantean memory democracy in action. And ... you gotta remain truthful you know, so it also functions as a chapter of Earthlings Anonymous — EA!"

"Ohmigod! Uncle Joe Zuvuya! You're going all the way with this one, aren't you?"

"You bet, Bud. Except if you're gonna say my whole name, remember it's 'Uncle Joe *13* Zuvuya.'" As he emphazed the '13' of his middle name, I could almost catch the glimpse of a vortex — ethereal, vibrant, elusive. Was *that* Uncle Joe? I wondered to myself.

"Feelin' the power of the 13, huh? But you'd better snap back in, Bud," Uncle Joe broke my revery, "or that next wave is gonna leave you way behind! The stakes are high this time around. As high as they've ever been for this stage of the evolutionary plunge."

"I'll buy that, Uncle Joe. But tell me what it means — the Crystal Earth whatever Network. Tell me how it works."

"OK. Every functioning Home Improvement Association chapter of 12 members becomes a Crystal Earth node. The purpose of the Crystal Earth Network is to generate *energy* and to link up with every other Association chapter of 12. When this starts to happen, you've got the beginning formation of a Crystal Earth Energy Network — like a crystal grid spread over the planet.

"I'll give you a tip on how to generate the energy. Work in groups of three. Form triangles. In any group of 12 you've got four main groups of three. And it doesn't matter who the people are. We're dealing in humans, not in roles people

play. Rather than looking at roles, look at talent pools —
from poetry to plumbing. But it's the human-to-human
energy hookups within the triangles that are important.
So, be bold! And remember: you can work in as many
triangles as you need to. Even in a group of four people,
everyone's got three triangles to work with."

"Triangles, huh? Doesn't that bring up sex, Uncle Joe?"

"Sure does. Didn't think we were going to leave sex out
of this did you, Bud? I know you too well, hee hee hee!"

"Watch it, Uncle Joe. You're getting out my dirty laundry."

"Hey, Bud! You're the one who said it!"

"OK, Uncle Joe, OK. What about sex?"

"Let it out and let it rip! But since you're all nervous
about AIDS — and I don't blame you, at least given what
you presently know — you've got to figure out some other
way to get off on that energy. You've got to get cosmically
horny and have wave-rippling cosmic orgasms."

"Cosmic orgasms!" What had Uncle Joe been doing up
at the AA Midway Station?

"Yep. Cosmic orgasms. That's what happens when three
people are playing consciously as a triangle of energies. I
can't tell you anymore. You gotta try it. And remember,
leave your answers — and your name — at the door."

Cosmically horny! I had to sit with that one for a minute.
Suddenly, I got an image of a triangle drawn on the ground.
The triangle then turned into a pyramid — a three-sided
one, not including the base on the ground, so that the
pyramid was actually a tetrahedron. Up above the place in
the pyramid where all the points met, I saw a hotline, like
a stream of lightning or fire pouring down from someplace
higher up. When the stream of lightning fire hit the point
at the top of the pyramid, the whole thing lit up, and the
stream of fire ran around and connected every point in the
pyramid. This whole image came in the batting of an eyelid.

"Wow," I said aloud. "What was that?"

"Oh, don't mind that, Bud. That's one of those Mayan optical exercises. You actually do those to stir up your memory. Let's not get sidetracked.

"What I've told you about so far is just for starters. There's ongoing stuff, too. That's the Home Improvement Association part.

"See, you got your house and you got your environment — the yard. Your house is your body and everything that goes along with it — from what you put into it to what you think and feel. Your yard is the planet. That's what you've got to improve in whatever way you can so your house and your yard work together.

"First thing you gotta do is clean 'em up. You know what a mess it is now. There's no self-discipline. You got unruly tenants — ego-tripping bums everyone of 'em. Just like on TV at one of those official government hearings. Everyone's trying to defend themselves. Can't have that kind of stuff in this kind of Home Improvement Association. That's why these Association chapters are also chapters of Earthlings Anonymous."

"Earthlings Anonymous, Uncle Joe? You mentioned that earlier. Say more."

"Yep. Earthlings Anonymous — EA. That's how you keep yourselves straight. Everyone tells the truth. Everyone owns up to their powerlessness over their human habits, and to how they've been giving their power away; giving it over to those dirty ego-swindlers. So the first step in EA goes: *We admitted we were powerless over our human habits and the disempowering institutions we created to support them.* That's basic. If you don't get to that one, you haven't even started to play."

"Catch a wave, Uncle Joe, that's perfect!"

"Not only is it perfect, Bud, but it's the way you get

your cleanup campaign going — your Campaign for the
Earth. You get all those Crystal Earth Energy Network Home
Improvement Associations linked up as a collective, then
you're dealing in real power. Then you've got your next step."

"Next step from what?"

"Next step from Harmonic Convergence. Wasn't that
your concern, Bud?"

"Right. So the next step from Harmonic Convergence is . . ."

". . . to harmonic detergents," Uncle Joe completed my
sentence with a side-splitting cackle. Where did this guy
come from? I could see a big box of galactic laundry soap,
Hunab Ku Tide, being emptied over the planet, iridescent
bubbles swirling up from the dirty water.

Calming himself down, Uncle Joe asked, "So you want
to get serious again. OK, then let's get to the Earth diving.
You want to know how that fits in to all of this too, right?"

"You're the boss, Uncle Joe."

"I thought the Boss was some musician you got down
there now."

"No, Uncle Joe. This is no time for bad puns."

"Why not? Pun's a pun. 'Once a pun on time . . . ,' is
the way all Mayan fairy tales begin."

"Uncle Joe! Behave!"

"So what is it about Earth diving that you want to know?"

"Go over it again. Where does it come from? How does
it fit into the Home Improvement Association — the Crystal
Earth Energy Network?"

"If you want to know the truth, it's an engineering project
that Layf-Tet-Tzun himself is supervising. It involves the
Home Improvement Association directly. It also involves
us — the Dimensional Doubles Progressive Field Association.
It's the way our two Associations can work together. You see,
once you've got your Atlantean memory democracy going,
then something the third and fourth dimensionals do in

common is Earth diving. Have you tried it yet, Bud?"

"I've been trying to do it, Uncle Joe. I know it's important, especially if we're going to get the Earth's point of view. I mean, when it comes to pollution and environmental things, we ask all the experts but we never ask the Earth. And even though most of the 'experts' would think it was crazy to ask the Earth what *she* thinks, I know the Earth has an answer. So I'm trying it, Uncle Joe . . ."

"And?"

"Well, Uncle Joe. I'm not sure if I'm getting it."

"So tell me what you're doing, José."

"My technique is the siesta, Uncle Joe. When I take a siesta, I tell you to go Earth diving while I go into a . . . well it's not really sleep and it's not really dreaming. And I visualize this matrix, like a three-dimensional checkerboard, down in the core and I tell you to go there and find our little . . ."

"Node?" Uncle Joe filled in for me.

"Right. Our little node. And I tell you to take an energy beam or light beam from the node in the core up to the surface of the Earth, where I am — or should I say, where your real estate is resting quietly. But I'm not sure it's actually happening. I mean it's easy enough to visualize, Uncle Joe, but is it really working?"

"Good start, Bud. But sounds like you need it to be more active. You've gotta be more involved, right?"

"That's it, Uncle Joe," I could feel a ray of warmth or compassion flooding my body. "I've gotten glimpses of what's happening, and it seemed that the other day I could see some deep, intense blue lights while my body lay there relaxing. It seemed that I was getting some glimpses of actually passing down through the Earth. But I feel I need to know more about where I'm going and what this is accomplishing."

"I understand," Uncle Joe resumed in his reassuring manner. "Where you're going, or actually where *I'm* going, is into the core of the Earth. But it's not like what you think it is. Of course, anything you think you've got figured out in just the physical dimension is not going to be what you think it is. What's down there is an inter-dimensional chamber. At least that's what they call it upstairs. It's interdimensional because it's like a giant crystal. Crystals are like doorways between dimensions. You see them in the third dimension. But they're filled with all these simultaneous perspectives, and mysterious holograms of spectral light — you know, those iridescent colors, and *resonant* properties that connect them to the fourth dimension. It's like they're the hinge that swings you through the dimensions. Wheeee!"

Uncle Joe let off a sudden blast from his galactic kazoo, startling me into a state of super-wakefulness. This guy really gets around, I thought, but he never lets you off the hook. For a moment I felt really glad that Uncle Joe had come into my life as intensely as he had.

"Anyway," he continued, not missing a beat, "that's the Earth's core, like a giant iron crystal emitting heavy electro-magnetic winds. These winds beat up against the outer core. Now, the outer core is like a heavy-duty metal plate — the original heavy-metal band, you might say, hee hee hee!" God, how corny he could get, laughing at his own jokes. "But this plate is actually a kind of inner Earth in the same way we usually think of the Earth. It has continents and mountains and valleys and even a kind of ocean, only these oceans are all vibrations.

"So there's this plate — the outer core — and beyond it is the mantle. That's what's between the core and the crust of the Earth. You followin' me, Bud?"

"Yeah, I think so, Uncle Joe," I nodded. His description

of the Earth sounded so different, and yet so vivid. "Go on," I commanded eagerly.

"So you have this crystal core," Uncle Joe went on, like some old college professor totally absorbed by his topic, "aligned along the north and south polar axis. It's aligned along this axis because the North and South Poles are the points of entry into the Earth. By that I mean that if you were travelling to this planet in the form of electromagnetic vibrations and you wanted to get to the heart of things, you'd hit the electromagnetic field of the planet — maybe 40,000 miles out — and work your way in to the radiation belts — maybe 11,000 miles out. Eventually you'd get discharged toward one of the poles, and, if you were lucky, you'd slide down the etheric column and end up at the crystal core."

"An *etheric* column? You mean like invisible, Uncle Joe?"

"Yep. There's actually an etheric column that runs right through from North Pole to South Pole. It's like an interdimensional electromagnetic tube or channel running from both poles into the crystal core. So this core is like a radio receiver. All the programs go through here. I mean the programs from the galactic beam, of course, and the sun and whatever else wants to communicate something — like maybe some of what you call UFOs, heh heh heh." The way Uncle Joe pronounced 'UFOs' gave me a shiver. Somehow I sensed that there were UFOs in the center of the Earth — right this very moment.

"Now you're catching a wave, Bud," Uncle Joe broke right into my mental drift. "You're certainly on to something. If you can access the Earth's core, you're accessing a mighty powerful computer as well. You see it's from here that Earth generates her programs."

"Is this where that Harmonic Convergence signal came from, Uncle Joe?"

"You bet. Just let me finish here and then let's see how
we can help you.

"So there at the core you've got this radio computer.
But the energy there is also intense and fierce. You gotta
remember that. It's dense and it's light all at once. It's kind
of like at the center of the sun. And it pulsates in rhythmic
patterns. It's like a heartbeat. Makes sense, doesn't it? Earth's
alive, so she's gotta have a heartbeat, right, Bud?"

"Of course, Uncle Joe," I replied, sensing the awesome
immensity of a being whose existence had been systematically
and publicly denied. How sad! This great Earth, treated like
a dead rock to be pillaged and ransacked. And yet how
alive, how undeniably real and alive she is. It was almost
as if I were picking up the Earth's heartbeat through my
. . . brain waves?

"That's right, Bud," Uncle Joe affirmed for me, "your
skull is a resonant plate, just like the Earth's outer core is a
resonant plate. This outer core picks up the heartbeats from
the crystal core. It mimics the surface of the Earth, and the
surface of the Earth mimics it. And your skull — it mimics
the whole show! Messages are sent back and forth between
the surface and outer core through a transferring medium,
which is also like an electromagnetic insulator. That's
the mantle."

"Wait a minute!" I cried out, feeling exasperated and
overloaded. "This Earth you're describing doesn't sound like
anything I ever heard of, Uncle Joe. It sounds like some
electrical engineer's idea of the Earth."

"That's not far from the truth, Bud. Electricity is the
fluid of the universe! It's the cosmic juice. Anyway, like I
said, when you look at things only one-dimensionally you
can't really see them for what they are. Layf-Tet-Tzun, Pacal
Votan . . . they're like electrical engineers or maybe electromagnetic engineers riding the galactic surf. It's not just the

electricity, but the electricity *and* the magnetism that give things their oomph!"

"What about gravity?"

"That's the force that holds things together. You know that, José. It's like love. In fact it *is* love. Love is a cosmic force. It juices the octaves running up and down the interdimensional channel. It's the energy that steps down information from one dimension to another. And once it has stepped that information down, it holds it together. It's not just something for Valentine's Day cards. If it weren't for love, we wouldn't be here."

"That's cool, Uncle Joe," I replied. "I get it, but I need more answers. How is all of this Layf-Tet-Tzun's engineering project? I mean the Earth diving?"

"OK. You get the picture of how it is down there. Now remember: I told you that you're a hologram of the Earth and vice versa. So if you've got your 'third-dimension physicals' grounding things on the crust through the Crystal Earth Energy Network Home Improvement Association, and you've got your Dimensional Doubles Progressive Field Association Earth diving and creating this grid in the Earth's crystal core, you've got some interesting little project going on. You've got cooperation between the dimensions *and* between the Earth and you. Think about that!

"See, the way this whole thing operates *is* Layf-Tet-Tzun's engineering project — I mean the Crystal Earth Energy Network and the Earth diving. One way or another, he figures, the Atlanteans will remember. If he can get them to actually become involved in the Earth, then everything will lighten up, and he'll be able to graduate! Good show, huh?"

"That's a big chunk, Uncle Joe. Let me sit on it a little," I answered, starting to feel a bit drowsy. I thought I was seeing things in front of my eyes. My ears were ringing more than usual, too. Was it too much information, or was it . . . an invitation to join Uncle Joe and go Earth diving? Fighting off sleep, I still had to get more information.

"Uncle Joe," I called out, afraid I might be losing contact, "this Campaign for the Earth sounds like an interdimensional strategy. While we're getting our atmospheric clean-up campaigns going through our EA Chapters and the Home Improvement Associations, the Earth diving is strengthening both the intelligence of the Earth — and ourselves."

"You got it, Bud. Another win-win synergism. Everyone wins, and everyone gets something good that nobody thought was there by doing it. You get your chapters going — your 12-person Crystal Earth Energy nodes — and pay some attention to this Earth diving, and you'll find out that you can pull the plug on what's keeping this mess going *and* have fun at the same time. How can you lose with that, Bud?"

There was no way I could answer. Sleep had overtaken me once again. Or was it sleep? I found myself spinning down what seemed like an endless vortex.

6
WHY
CRYSTALS
MATTER

 As I hurtled down the vortex, it seemed as if I was passing through layers and layers of some kind of substance — a time substance, and at the same time an Earth substance. Then I began to slow down. As my velocity diminished, I saw him — Uncle Joe. There he was, no longer a voice in my head, but the real McCoy!

He looked almost elfish, like a leprechaun, but he was transparent too. Was he Mayan? He had on a kind of jacket, and something that was not pants but more like pantaloons. His forehead was flat and angled like a Mayan's, and his hair was tied together and swept back almost like plumage. His clothes were iridescent. In fact, all of him seemed iridescent — pink around the edge and turquoise in the middle, but glowing. He held his left arm out, his forearm vertical so that his palm was facing me. His right arm was held downward, but again with his palm out and facing me. It looked like he was doing some kind of salute. He was barefoot, and crouched ever so slightly as if he were . . . surfing?

"Tables are turned, José," he grinned, relaxing his salute.

"How's that, Uncle Joe?"

"This time I'm here, but you're not."

"What?"

"Well, you can see me, but can you see yourself? Where are you?" As he spoke, Uncle Joe bent down into a low surfer's crouch, his arms out for balance, his hair blowing and billowing in some kind of wind that crackled and whooshed with enormous energy. "So where are *you*?" he asked again, determined to get an answer.

I looked around. There was no me, at least no body. Where was I? What was going on? Was I dreaming? How could I be dreaming? I looked at Uncle Joe again. How could I be looking? What was looking? Had I become a disembodied consciousness? Was I . . . dead? Where were these thoughts coming from?

"I don't know, Uncle Joe," I finally mustered up a response. My words sounded more like an echo than anything else. "I seem to be here, but I'm not. Yet you're here; I can see you. But how can I see you if I can't see myself? Who is seeing? What is seeing?"

Uncle Joe bent over in laughter. He was clearly getting a kick out of all of this. It didn't irritate me that he was laughing at my expense, but I did feel perplexed. At the same time, I didn't feel bad. In fact, if a disembodied consciousness can feel anything at all, it felt downright good. That was it! I was it! I was like the atmosphere around Uncle Joe, and the atmosphere felt good. It was warm, tropical, but different . . . iridescent.

"Well guess what, Sonny Boy," said Uncle Joe, pulling himself together, "you deserved a break. You've been working hard, especially with your Campaign for the Earth. But I know you wanted to have a more *conscious* experience of Earth diving. So here you are, for a change, in the fourth dimension, with me. This is where I hang out. Your body is back up there, sleeping like a babe."

"Back up where, Uncle Joe? Where are we?"

"Center of the Earth, Bud, where you've always wanted to go."

Center of the Earth! Hallelujah! I felt like a giant starburst. My awareness expanded out. It was as if I were in some giant crystal. Yes, a crystal chamber with soaring, shifting walls that were more like membranes than solid walls, quivering and iridescent, moving like shuttles on a loom. Everything was breathing, pulsing. It was brilliant, and hot; dense yet light. Passing through the membranes at random angles, and moving faster than lightning speed, were great currents of energy which seemed to be like sounds, and at the same time like fantastically moving parades of people or other beings.

"Is . . . is this the interdimensional crystal chamber, Uncle Joe?" I finally asked, my voice coming out of some infinitely small point that was dancing gyroscopically atop one of the energy currents. Desperately, I tried to get my bearings, holding on and letting go at the same time.

"You could say that, Bud, but hold on now; we're not really there yet. Keep your focus on the back of my head." Uncle Joe turned around suddenly, and bent into a really low crouch. Then we took off. It was like wind surfing. We bumped and flew over magnetic waves, and passed through the shifting, pulsing crystal membranes until Uncle Joe did a neat 180-degree turn and swiftly, but gracefully, came to a halt. "Take a look now, Bud."

Removing my focus from Uncle Joe, I took in the scene. Everything was compressed and dense, yet transparent. Fantastic crystal forms penetrated by spears of glowing iron spread out in every direction, moving, growing, changing very rapidly, and yet very clearly. All of this action came from some central area, but it was hard to tell where that might be since everything was so dynamic. It was as if the gravity here was constantly changing direction.

As my focus slowly worked its way towards what seemed like the center of all this action, I lost track of Uncle Joe. Where was he?

"Wheeeee! Holy Zuvuya and whomp my Kuxan Suuuuuuuummmmmmmmmmmm!"

There he was, spiralling downwards like a drunken sailor holding on to a column or a pole. But the pole must have been invisible. There was nothing there, and yet his arms were holding on to something as he spiralled madly down, his jacket fluttering, his hair flapping and breaking in the madcap plunge. When he finally halted, he just sat there, his legs spread-eagled, his arms still holding on to the invisible pole, his head slumped down on his chest. His shoulders were moving. He was giggling.

And then I noticed it: the grid, the matrix. It was fine, almost invisible, like a huge rectangular Tinker Toy model. The connecting rods were like threads of fast moving light, yet they were organic. It was awesome, yet delicate and fragile. From some of the connecting points, very fine threads of light shot outwards. These must have been the Earth divers' energy lines shooting back to the surface. But the whole matrix was transparent. Everything within and around it was moving. Nothing was stable. It was dizzying. Whatever consciousness I had left seemed to be ebbing away, dissolving into the matrix, into the crystal forms and the molten iron spears, all of it spinning like a kaleidoscope . . .

"Easy there, Dude." I could hear Uncle Joe's voice. "You got this far in your dream body, you don't want to lose it now." Where was he? I trained my focus on the echo of his words, but the echoes divided into other echoes, and it all started to dissolve again. Then I caught a pinpoint of light, an intense, electric blue light. I put my focus on that light until it suddenly opened up in the form of Uncle Joe Zuvuya. He was sitting now, cross-legged at the very middle of the matrix, his arms folded over each other across his chest. It looked like he had taken his jacket off. Now he completely appeared to be some ancient, timeless Mayan.

"Whew! What's going on, Uncle Joe?"

"Little gravity-vortex vertigo. Everyone gets it when they first come down here," he replied. Just looking at him sitting there cross-legged, his arms folded across his chest like Sitting Bull or a Buddha of some kind, calmed me down.

"Gravity-vortex vertigo?"

"Yeah. Gravity-vortex vertigo. You see, here at the center of the Earth the gravity waves are pulling everything in as tight as can be. Meanwhile you've got the electromagnetic energy coming down that pole you saw me sliding down. The electromagnetic energy from that pole interacts with the gravity waves so that it creates all these little vortices spinning out every which way from the center. These vortices are actually information spirals from the beam. The Earth literally channels the beam down its polar axis, and then when the energy hits center here — blam! Out it goes, inter- acting with the gravity waves which turn into all these crystal and molten iron forms."

"But why crystal, Uncle Joe?" I asked, fascinated by the changing liquid-crystal forms that were spurting in all directions.

"So now, José," his eyes narrowed as he looked at me, "you want to know why crystals are important — why they matter to people?" As Uncle Joe asked his question, it seemed as if a crystal throne was forming right beneath him, only to dissolve again into a river of molten iron. Unperturbed, he went on. "I know, a lot of you folks up there have been collecting crystals like mad lately. The reason why is this: crystals are like Earth's medicine. You've been collecting them because all of you are kind of off center. Your wave-forms are wobbly. And the crystals, well they come to you, actually. You attract them, like when a body gets sick it attracts the medicine to make it well."

"Crystals are like medicine, Uncle Joe? What do they do?"

"They vibrate at a very high rate of speed. They vibrate to your wave-form, and they cool out your wave-form. They bring messages and gather messages and hold messages. And these messages have to do with putting you back into harmony — harmony with yourself and harmony with the Earth. Because it's the *Earth* that produces them. From Earth's point of view, there's nothing more common than quartz crystal. But to the Earth these quartz crystals, and all their crystalline relatives, are like information or intelligence nodes, or even neurons! Each one is special, and yet each one contains the hologram of the Earth. But that's the point. The Earth mother is a crystal planet."

"The Earth a crystal planet! Now that's something, Uncle Joe," my voice popped enthusiastically out of its dancing pinpoint of disembodied consciousness.

"You got it, José. That's how come you've got to take care of crystals and use them properly. People think, 'Oh, that's just a piece of rock.' But then they forget, Earth's alive, this rock's alive. Concentrate on those little suckers. Put your highest intention into them. Look deep inside of them. Listen to them. They're sensitive to you. You can also think of them as Earth's memory and intelligence probes seeking you out. See, a crystal is Earth's way of reclaiming another human. So surrender when one finds you. They keep you in tune with the Earth, and vice versa. Fact is, each one of those crystals is a spirit helper, an Earth ally. One other thing."

"What's that, Uncle Joe?"

"You're lucky, damned lucky. You know why?"

"Beats me, Uncle Joe. What do you have up your sleeve?"

"It's not so much what I've got up my sleeve. It's more like right now you don't have any sleeves at all. And even if you did, you've got no arms to put in them. Hee hee hee! In fact you're not even here at all. That's the point."

I had to grant that Uncle Joe was right. I wasn't there at all, except that I was — at least my consciousness was there.

"You got it," Uncle Joe continued. Still seated cross-legged, he was grinning as wide as can be. "That's why you're so lucky. You're getting to experience this through your dream body — me! Not everybody's that lucky. Most people aren't hooked up to their dream bodies, so they can't have this kind of experience — yet. But they will, if they play their cards right."

"How are they supposed to play their cards, Uncle Joe?"

"Easy, Bud: by dealing straight! And they do that first by getting their Crystal Earth Energy Network Home Improvement Associations together, by cleaning up their act, cleaning up the Earth, and, taking care of their crystals. There's a payoff to all that, and the payoff is getting hooked up with their dream bodies."

"So before the dream lights up, we've all got to pull together and do this thing right, huh, Uncle Joe?"

"Sure. And have fun with those crystals!" Uncle Joe's voice began to fade. A great rushing, roaring sound grew louder and louder, until it filled everything. It became all that there was — sheer, white, crystal-powered noise — awesome, like the sun exploding inside the Earth.

My focus wandered jaggedly through the immensity of the noise, which was like brilliant, mirrored, crystal light. At the same time, it was intense, and filled with fleeting iridescent images.

Then another noise set in. My focus expanded from

one, to two, to three, until it finally settled on what seemed like eight portals or cave-like holes. As amazing as this might seem, my focus was simultaneously set on all eight of these portals, which extended outward in every direction from the center. It was from these portals that this next noise was coming, like a great number of voices speaking or chanting all at once.

Uncle Joe was still seated as calm as ever at the center of all this.

"What's happening, Uncle Joe? What's all this noise about?" I asked.

"That first big rush, well, that was like a burp — a big post-Harmonic Convergence Earth burp. You might call it an energy swell that's gotta get released. Might be some good dreams up there for the land folks."

As Uncle Joe spoke, I kept my focus on the eight portals. What was going on there? Through each portal I could see swirls of people or beings of some kind, all transparent like Uncle Joe. Everything was now white and bright inside the interdimensional chamber, except for the portals, which became more and more distinct. There was one portal at each pole, two that were far to either side of Uncle Joe, and four others that extended out from a couple of invisible axes located where Uncle Joe was sitting.

"You should listen carefully, Bud. You might hear something mighty interesting," Uncle Joe nodded as he spoke.

So I tried to listen, and at the same time to get a clearer focus on what was going on inside those portals. I started to hear something I could understand: words that sounded like a weird kind of poetry.

"Who are you?" I asked, trying to direct my voice to all eight portals at once.

"We are the energy beings," the answer came back in a great chorus. "We are the electromagnetic keepers of the

Earthly records."

"What? Energy beings? Earthly records?"

Then, from several of the portals, a few of these energy beings came out. They were hard to see and kept turning around very quickly, as if each one was vibrating rapidly on its own axis. Some of them looked female, others male, but it was really hard to tell.

"Yes, we are energy beings. The Earthly records are the ledgers of all the actions and intentions of you humans. But let us tell you something."

"What's that?"

"We who call ourselves energy beings are the same ones that you once called gods. The gods were never more than us, and we are nothing more than the intention of the Earth to be mirrors or reflectors of what you are."

"But," I asked astonished, "what are you all doing down here?"

"We are down here renewing ourselves. As you know, on the Earth among you humans, it is now, and has been for quite some time, a time of darkness. You have been creating a dark spell. As you separated more and more from your light bodies, you became more and more clever at inventing toys and creating material wealth for yourselves. As this happened, more and more of you found less and less use for us. In the pride you took in your cleverness, you did not notice how dark it had become. You came to think that your light bodies, your souls, were a superstition of the past. So we came down here to regroup."

As the echoing chorus of words was released, the beings appeared to vibrate faster and faster, becoming scarcely more than swirls of energy. Then the voices continued, sounding almost like a soprano chorus: very feminine, but haunting, and as if coming from a great distance. This chorus was, in fact, the most haunting thing I had ever

heard in my life. It was so sad and haunting that I thought
I could have died just from the terrible sweetness of it all.
Were these the muses of the gods that I was hearing?

"But now the time is approaching when either we are
summoned back and recognized again or we must pass up
the polar axis and go elsewhere. We have waited for so long
now. We have waited this entire baktun. We have kept the
records of your terrible wars and the things you are doing
to one another. We are happy that the Atlantean memory
is being awakened, the Atlantean memory of victory and
destruction and future hope, and that you are setting up
a memory grid down here. That will help.

"But time is short and we are full of nothing but goodness
for everybody. However we must be summoned; we must
be called; we must be beckoned; we must be invoked; for
we are the gods, the spirits of the Earth, the energy beings
who fulfill desire. Appease us with the prayer and smoke
offerings that call to us through the smell of sage and juniper;
draw us into your circles — soon. For if we are not called
and must therefore depart, then the terrible storm of Earth's
wrath will fall everywhere. If we depart, it would be like
you as a human losing your brain, your memory, your ability
to be conscious, to sing, to experiment, to dare . . ."

The chorus dissolved into a high pitched sound that
echoed and reverberated everywhere. It was eery, no doubt
about it. Slowly the noise died down and strange dancing
lights bounced back and forth between the different portals.
I looked for my familiar point of reference, Uncle Joe, but
he was no longer seated at the center of this bizarre ever-
changing space. Where had he gone?

"Over here, Bud!"

My attention went to the upper portal, the one situated
on the axis. Uncle Joe was seated on the edge of the portal,
his legs and bare feet dangling down — if there could be

such a direction as down at the center of the Earth.

"You've still got a few dream-credits left, Bud. You can use them up by doing some more electromagnetic windsurfing with me. How 'bout it?"

Why hesitate? So far this was the best payoff I had ever had. This fantastic adventure would give me enough energy and inspiration to keep me going for a long, long time.

"Sure, Uncle Joe, where to?" My focus was now on Uncle Joe's head and shoulders. I could see the funny iridescent hairs curling out of his ears and nostrils.

"Well, there's someone else you might want to meet."

"Who's that, Uncle Joe?"

"How 'bout Layf-Tet-Tzun?"

"Wow, Uncle Joe! Really? That's some exciting prospect. But here we are at the center of the Earth, and I thought old Layf-Tet-Tzun was up in Alcyone, the Central Sun."

"That's true, Bud. But don't forget about the Mayan walkie-talkie system, the Kuxan Suum."

"The Kuxan Suum, Uncle Joe, for sure, the Kuxan Suum, that's how I got here in the first place, right?"

"You bet, José. That Kuxan Suum fiber extending out of your solar plexus is your interdimensional lifeline. It'll vibrate you anywhere, as long as your intention is pure and you know what you're doing. Nowadays there's not many of you humans who've got that together. But like I said, you're just plain lucky. Here now, hitch onto my hair and let's go . . . Wheeee!" In a twinkling we were off and sailing, speeding with tremendous velocity through great waves of light.

"Lucky, Uncle Joe?" I asked as we hurtled through crystal clouds and time warps. "When you say that, Uncle Joe, I get the feeling you're doing me some kind of favor, or else playing a joke on me."

"Both, José. You know, as your official Guardian Angel

I've saved your life more than once. That one time when I kept you from falling off the subway track dead drunk, you kind of got that *maybe* I was around. But if I was just doing you favors, it would go to your head. That's how come I also engineer a few jokes into your life situation. Like those couple times you lost your job. Hee hee hee!"

Settling into my discomfort, I contented myself with the spectacular scenery, if you could call it that, through which we wailed and roared. Great fiery discs blew like snowflakes through a tunnel of shimmering membrane walls. We sailed over several fleets of luminous jellyfish-shaped objects that were emitting rapidly rotating light beams. At one point a giant doughnut-shaped object, enclosing a massive circular light harbor, loomed into view. It had docking points for dozens, or even hundreds, of the jellyfish-shaped objects.

Picking up on my curiosity, Uncle Joe cried out through the roaring, warbling whoosh of the Kuxan Suum's electromagnetic surf, "That's the AA Midway Station, Bud. You scarcely have enough dream-credits to get to Layf-Tet-Tzun, but I'll buzz you through the monitor banks. That way we won't disrupt any of the meetings going on down there."

As we approached the fabled AA Midway Station, I could make out a vertical, doughnut-shaped, light form intersecting the more visible horizontal form with its light harbor and docking points. The vertical form was twinkling with all sorts of little lights that moved rapidly in no apparent pattern. It appeared that we were headed for the vertical form.

"Hold on, now! We're just gonna whiplash through, Bud," Uncle Joe called out as we entered a small light hole towards the top of the massive form.

The inside of the light form was spectacular: a semicircular bank of what appeared to be rows and rows of TV screens, each one with a different scene. But what scenes! Strange colored landscapes, microscopic visions of fire cells,

crystal cities, swirling green dust-tornadoes, subaquatic
star colónies. It was awesome, and it seemed endless. And
then it was gone. We passed through another light porthole
and were rapidly Kuxan-Suum-sailing across the electromagnetic ether.

"Sorry we couldn't linger, José. But that gives you a
taste. There's a lotta stuff going on in this galaxy, lotta
stuff your scientist friends could know about and should
know about if only they accepted again the reality of other
dimensions. Course, that would change their ... whoaaa!"
Uncle Joe cut himself off in midsentence and appeared to
slow down a bit. Before us was a gigantic globe of fiery
light. "Alcyone, the Central Sun!" Uncle Joe shouted
triúmphantly.

Because of our speed, the globe rapidly grew in size until
it became all there was. The heat must have been intense,
but I felt nothing. We passed through several layers of fiery
substance and then arrived at what appeared to be a huge
transparent dome. Towards the bottom of the dome was a
large circular entryway. Passing through that, we encountered
something that was similar to a spiral escalator. It went up,
and at the same time it went deeper within. Along the way
there were transparent hexagonal billboards with floating
luminous geometrical forms arranged in different patterns.
They looked as if they were flashing some kind of code.

Then the spiral-escalator-like object came to an end.
Another circular doorway awaited us. Uncle Joe Zuvuya
paused. I could feel him straightening himself up, like he
was going to meet "The Boss." Pulling his jacket down, and
sweeping his hands back over his plumage-like hair bundle,
Uncle Joe marched through the circular doorway. It was
magnificent inside. It was also oddly reminiscent of the
central core of the Earth, only this was much more majestic.
Giant walls of fiery crystalline forms sloped up all around

the central dome. But these crystalline forms were shaped in such a way that they also seemed to be like furniture, with all sorts of little places to sit or rest. However they weren't really that either, because there was nothing solid. They were more like holograms, but holograms that you could hear and smell as well as see.

In the middle of all this splendor, another staircase went up to an inner level. As we climbed this staircase, I could see a giant semicircular control board, like the one in a massive recording or TV studio. Beams of multicolored light flashed and sparkled in every direction from this board. These lights were similar to neon lasers, shooting off in intermittent beams almost like signals or code forms. The colors were intense — more intense than the primary colors red or green; they were turquoise and magenta — electrical pastels. Sometimes the lights would create great showers, and then burst in all directions. I had never seen anything like it before. The uncanny thing was that it all seemed so ... intelligent ... so intentional ... as if it were some kind of language, yet random.

Suddenly I became aware of a luminous form so transparent as to be almost invisible. Slowly this form turned toward us. Uncle Joe made a little bow and then gave the same salute he had given me when I first saw him: left arm up, right arm down, palms facing outward.

The luminous etheric form had a transparent, jellyfish quality to it, and yet appeared almost mineral. It was shaped something like a bell, tapering to a fine point at the top. Towards the top, which I presumed was the head, there were three horizontal bars — the only distinguishing feature of this etheric body.

"Greetings!" A voice came right from inside of wherever I was. "I am very old. And I am the only one remaining. The Layf-Tet-Tzun you see here soon must leave." The voice echoed itself, but continued with great dignity. It also had an old, tired, almost absent-minded quality to it. "Once I was many, but now we are one. And now many must come to replace this one. It is too much for this self and my projected helper to monitor all of the beams. I, Layf-Tet-Tzun, the Keeper of the Central Sun, Alcyone, also called Lamat, am ready for the higher light dimensions. So please, carry out my project! Let those who dive into the Earth be ready to replace this ancient one. If all goes well, I shall send my emissary to inspect and give further instruction. But now I must return . . . to my work."

The voice faded and crackled. The luminous ancient form turned and settled itself down at the center of the massive control board. Then, as if from the center of Layf-Tet-Tzun's light body, another much smaller body suddenly came into focus. Like Layf-Tet-Tzun's body, this one was also bell-shaped. But it had more substance, and more of a head. In fact, from this pumpkin-shaped head, a little crystal-like form emitted a beam of ever-changing colors that hit the control board at different places. As it did so, an awesome music arose and filled the space with thunderous majestic tones, echoing and building on each other.

Awestruck at the spectacle, I whispered to Uncle Joe, "Is that little guy Layf-Tet-Tzun's projected helper and emissary?"

"Yeah," Uncle Joe replied. "Old LT, he's in the fifth dimension. The helper, LT Junior, is all that LT's got left for the fourth dimension. That's how come LT's waiting for the Atlanteans to graduate and come here in their fourth-dimensional light bodies and get a whole other evolutionary round going. That way, LT can graduate, too."

As Uncle Joe spoke, I strained to get a better look at the helper, LT Junior. Then, as if picking up my thought-wave, the helper-emissary turned toward us. A small, round, but slightly oblong head was perched atop the transparent flowing bell- or jellyfish-shaped body. There were no arms or legs. The bottom of the body appeared to be in flames, as if a robe had caught fire, but the flames stayed in the same position.

I went back to the head. It was so simple and ancient in feeling. Two very large ears ending in little elfinlike points were on either side of it. The only feature on the front of this head was a long, mouthlike slit. Inside the mouth-slit were what seemed to be flashing sensory devices. At the top of the head was a diamond pattern, in the middle of which was an organic crystal device which emitted the beams that hit the control board.

Giving us a nod, LT Junior returned to work. The boards flashed with multicolored beams. The sounds reached new crescendos. Then suddenly, everything vanished.

We rushed back through the electromagnetic surf. Becoming dizzy as we spiralled through the endless membranes of light, the last thing I remember Uncle Joe saying was, "OK, José, you're on your own. You've used up your last dream credits for now. Time to spiral you back into that sleeping babe you call your body."

As Uncle Joe gently guided my conscious energy back to where my body was sleeping, I felt the understanding of dream credits come to me along with a deepened sense of love and caring from Uncle Joe.

"Yeah, Bud," Uncle Joe's voice echoed from within the dream that my body was now having, "dream credits. They're just the bonuses you get for letting your dimensional double run interference for you!" Somehow that seemed terribly funny, and in a wavelike burst of dream-laughter, I could see Uncle Joe zig-zagging through a vortex, his arms held in that Mayan pose he had used when I had first seen him, everything in his wake becoming calm and serene like the ocean at sunrise before it has been swept by the rippling currents of the day's first wind . . .

7

ZEN OF
THE CLEAN
WAVE-FORM

 Grounded. Down to Earth. It certainly felt good after that last mind-altering, reality-adjusting, cosmically co-creating trip! Uncle Joe did not come around much after that. But I knew where he was. He was up at the Arcturus-Antares Midway Station attending more of his postgraduate 12-step meetings.

"Cleanup time goes for everybody, at all levels and dimensions, Bud," Uncle Joe whispered to me at one point. "You got enough to do and think about for now, what with Earthlings Anonymous, the Home Improvement Association, and Earth diving. So let me get back to cleaning up my act. When we meet again we're gonna be polished!"

Why should I complain if Uncle Joe left me? It was only temporary. And like Uncle Joe had said, I was lucky. Besides, I had learned a long time ago that after the vision comes the hard work. What I had to do now was to settle into my wave-form, and take another look at this whole Mayan thing.

Parking my body next to central channel, I entered a meditation, or a vertical tune-up as Uncle Joe calls it. It

was time to let the love-force that was running the vertical
octaves assemble all my loose parts and get my alignment
to Uncle Joe up to speed. "Radical," I could hear Uncle Joe
saying, "you've got to get radical, back to the roots, your
roots." So my mind travelled back . . .

You know, I used to think I had begun this Mayan
adventure when I was a fourteen-year-old Mexican-American
kid looking for his roots. When I was that age, a climb up
the pyramids outside of Mexico City had had a profound
impact on me. Soon after this I learned about the calendar
and the mystery of the Maya themselves. I knew there was
something to that calendar, the 260-unit module called the
Tzolkin. So I pressed myself into it, or, like a seal into wax,
it pressed itself into me. I read about it, thought about it,
and dreamed about it. I even drew it and painted it. I studied
the prophecies related to it, and what was left of the ancient
texts. I traveled back and forth to the Yucatan.

Sometime over the last few years, as I prepared for
Harmonic Convergence, it started to dawn on me: I have
known about this stuff longer than I have been alive. When
I saw that the answer to the Mayan mystery was to be found
out in the galaxy, it was as if I had been flipped head over
heels and lit on fire. I poured all of my knowledge and intuition into *The Mayan Factor*. As my Uncle Joe Zuvuya will
attest, I was slam-dunked into infinity, if for no other reason
than to come up with the phrase "Harmonic Convergence."

But if I was slam-dunked into infinity, then infinity was
also slam-dunked into me. And since genetically I am no
different than anyone else, hasn't everyone else also had
this knowledge longer than they have been alive?

Being slam-dunked into infinity is nothing more than
waking up to the fact that your memory — your total database, including your genetic program — has been operating
longer than you have had your name. For instance, you

must have a thought about the microchip before you can create a microchip. And, of course, the information that a specific microchip accommodates, which is similar to the body you now have, also exists before the microchip is made. It's like Uncle Joe says: there's an electrical and cosmic design or code that everything comes from — you, me, the computer, the planet, the sun, and the galaxy. The Mayan contribution to all of this, I had discovered, was the Tzolkin, the master microchip design and database, the interdimensional index and ratio.

In physics there is the periodic table of elements, which is a list of all the elements from hydrogen to uranium, including all the rare elements, and their atomic weights and isotope numbers. This is technical information, but it is very useful if we want to understand and create and recreate the physical plane, the third dimension.

Well, the Tzolkin is similar to this periodic table except that it is the periodic table of interdimensional galactic frequencies. Just as there are 144 elements, there are 260 galactic frequencies. And just as the periodic table of elements gets us through the third dimension, the Tzolkin allows us to play interdimensional handball — while we are cresting a wave, no less!

The Tzolkin is like the master microchip. It is the 260-unit galactic constant. As the galactic constant, the Tzolkin is the cosmically electrical design code. Its code allows for the design of any kind of wave-form, in any dimension. And because it is modular, the Tzolkin is the gauge or measure of the wave-form — my wave-form, your wave-form, or any wave-form. It works like a building code. If the wave-form is not up to specs, it does not get hooked-up. And if it doesn't get hooked-up, well, it just doesn't go anywhere. As Uncle Joe says, it doesn't even make it to the now — that's worse than a flat tire before you've turned on the ignition.

Your wave-form is the sum total of your programs, your genetic program as well as your electromagnetic vibrational frequency. You know you are electromagnetic, for instance, when you get those sexual tingles. Anyway, your wave-form is your own unique vibrational frequency. That's why the Galactic Scouts say, "Know your vibration; by my vibration shall you know me, and by their vibration shall you know them."

The fact is, way deep down, everybody *knows* their own vibrations, and they know what they vibrate to. And as everybody also knows, they have got to keep feeling those good vibrations.

By its nature, a vibration is a frequency wave. Your frequency wave is a form, because any frequency that vibrates for any amount of time can be mapped. It can be drawn on a graph. The mapping of any frequency is its form. In fact, all geometrical forms are mappings of different frequencies. A circle is one frequency pattern, a square is another, and a hexagon still another.

When you get together with someone, either your wave-forms mesh or they don't. Or maybe they just neutralize each other. So it's not just chemistry. The chemistry is just the juicy stuff that happens once the wave-forms have registered each other.

What all this means is that even though each individual wave-form is slightly different from every other wave-form, there is a common denominator, a wave-form model that is encoded in the Tzolkin, the galactic constant.

As the galactic constant, the Tzolkin encodes light frequencies, crystalline frequencies, and genetic frequencies. Light frequencies are electromagnetic energy patterns. Crystalline frequencies describe the elements and forms of matter. Genetic frequencies refer to organic life patterns. Of course they are all intermixed. Take humans for example. As beautiful as they think they are, their beauty is really the result of a particular combination of 64 DNA codons. These codons are the amino acid "code words" of the genetic code. These little six-part structures come together to create the twisting double-helix patterns that we associate with DNA. These patterns, in their particular combinations, contain the information that translates into what we *think* is our physical beauty. "If you humans would stop taking credit for your beauty," Uncle Joe told me once, "then your beauty would really shine!"

Naturally, the DNA code is described as having its own vibratory structure. Our genes vibrate. So whatever our particular genetic combinations may be, they determine our particular wave-forms. Yet, despite apparent differences, and our imperfections, everyone is made up of the same stuff. Each one of us contains the very same code that describes the pattern of all the other wave-forms.

The Mayans say, "In Lake'ch," "I am another yourself." We are all the same human. In and through myself I know you and you know me. Sounds like a good reason to be tolerant and compassionate, doesn't it?

Not only is each human its own unique wave-form, but all of humanity is a single wave-form. We could think of humanity as a wave that is moving and growing in time. And of course the Earth is its own wave-form, as the Sun and solar system are their own wave-forms, and the galaxy itself is one big crystal wave-form that encompasses and recapitulates all the lesser wave-forms. Waves within waves. Waves giving rise to waves. Everything in motion within the galactic ocean!

Yes, the galactic ocean! Did you ever stop to think about it? Beams and rays emitting sparkling prismatic drops of electromagnetic spray, star systems, planets, mineral forma-

tions dazzling in color and shape, and the life forms —
innumerable waves, writhing and twisting their way through
geometries of time, filling every possible space with ingenious
constructs, thought forms, wavelengths — seeking and
surfing their way back along the Zuvuya to the source . . .

Now, if all of these wave-forms are regulated by the
interdimensional galactic constant, the Tzolkin, it means that
your own wave-form is ultimately the echo of the galactic
wave-form. But an echo — isn't that the same as a memory?

Zingggg! That high-pitched sound you just heard in
your ear — was it an echo? A memory wave of the stars?
Who are you really? Or better yet, *what* are you? Where
do you begin and where do you end? If your body, including
its wave-form, is a galactic memory, who are you anyway?
And if your unique wave-form is a distant echo of the galactic
wave-form, who knows what memories you really have
stored in that high density frequency pack you call yourself?

Then there is the galactic beam — how does it play into
all of this? How does it help shape your wave-form?

The acceleration-synchronization beam which the Maya
came here to measure is regulated by the galactic constant,
the Tzolkin. That means that the beam's different frequency
cycles and patterns can be measured or modulated by different
ratios of the interdimensional 260-unit Tzolkin. That also
means that all the wave-forms affected by the beam, including
those of your dog and your cat, are also regulated by the
Tzolkin. Like a cosmic tapestry weaving itself through your
sense experiences, the beam textures your wave-forms with
patterns from the Tzolkin!

A sound that carries over a long distance can only be
picked up by a receiver that is made to accommodate the
sound. Wave-forms are the receivers that pick up the "sound"
of the beam. The beam regulates the frequencies so that
different wave-forms respond in their own unique ways and

at the same time in their own absolutely cosmic ways. This is what allows your cat and yourself to have those mystical moments of total trust and time-stand-stillness.

This also means that the DNA from which we are created is in some divine way matched to the frequencies of the beam. The cosmic tapestry continues to weave itself, and to be woven by all of us. According to Uncle Joe, our knowledge of the beam is going to make "Star Trek" look like child's play by the time we get our vertical channels hooked-up in the "beam dreamtime of 2012."

Now, closely related to the idea of the wave-form is the concept of the hologram. A hologram is a structure of a wave-form reproduced three-dimensionally during any one instant of time. For example, you probably remember exactly where you were when you heard about the *Challenger* exploding. Then on television, the hologram of the moment was recreated over and over again.

If we could actually step outside of our relatively thick skulls and see ourselves as flows in time, we would see that each one of us is an ongoing wave-form. As in a film strip, this wave-form could be broken down into different frames. At any instant, each frame would show this wave-form to be based on a single hologram — myself, or what I think I am, or yourself, or what you believe you are.

"Hey José," Uncle Joe zapped in on the wisp of a vortex, "The faster you go hoppin' through those holograms, the faster they catch up with you! Think about it. Hee hee hee!" That old rascal, he just can't leave me alone.

The point of this is that all we are ever doing is recreating our own hologram. In fact, we can't get away from it. It is all we can do anyway. So we might as well just relax and become who we are! With whom and with what are we competing, anyway? We can't run faster than our own holograms. So we need to settle back and relax into what

we have always been. That way we can get more mileage
out of our Zuvuya circuit.

That's right, back to the Zuvuya. If we ask what it is
that gives continuity to our wave-forms, and what it is that
strings our different holograms together through time to create
our ongoing wave-forms, it's the Zuvuya circuit. Remember,
the Zuvuya circuit is our memory hotline. But memory
in this sense is not just recalling what we were doing the
first time we heard our favorite songs. On the Zuvuya circuit,
memory is the sum recollection of each of our unique
wave-forms, past *and* future, as well as the total galactic
wave-form of which each of us is a microchip reflection.

The key, of course, to using or tuning into the Zuvuya,
is to have a clean wave-form. Aha! So here's the rub. Clean
wave-form: no old limitations or hang-ups, past-life fears,
ego trips, competition, control, separateness — the whole
bag of tricks, wiped out by a clean wave-form! You see, all
of this talk about wave-forms is not just to give us something
new to think about. And it does not invalidate what we
already know about our physical anatomy. It is to show us
that we are more than what we think we are. Or, to be
precise, it is to show us that we are more than what we
think our third-dimensional body restricts us to being.

Being *more* than we are means that we are both an
electromagnetic wave-form *and* a reflection or recollection
of the interdimensional galactic wave-form. In other words,
we are ourselves and at the same time we are a walking
cosmic memory field. How star-trippingly delightful!

So, having a clean wave-form is knowing how to make
the most of this situation. It is important to know this if
we are really going to participate in Earthlings Anonymous.
That's right, now we're back to Earthlings Anonymous, or
EA. This also gets us to the Zen part. Right — Zen. From
Zen to Zuvuya — that's an important part of the Galactic

Scouts training manual.

The Zen part is knowing how to clean and take care of our wave-forms. But to do that, we first have to see that we have something to clean. And to see that, we have to be honest with ourselves: we have to be able to do that fearless moral inventory. We have to see ourselves as *clean*.

This is the nitty gritty of it all, the Zen of it. Yeah, Zen. It's nothing exotic. It is just the art of being in the now, and all the tricks it takes to do this. According to Zen, if we know how to hang out in the now at all times, we are keeping ourselves clean, but good!

"Hey Bud!" there he was again, the rascal.

"I thought this was my meditation, Uncle Joe!"

"Your meditation? Hmmph. I thought there was just meditation, the big wave, the Zuvuya that you tune into, and now you're calling it *your* meditation?"

Chagrined, I answered, "Thanks, Uncle Joe. You caught me just as I thought I was really getting hot. But what was it you were going to say?"

"That stuff about the now. That's great — only way to be in your hologram and channel the beam, if you know what I mean. Anyway, Bud,I was just gonna say that the best thing about hanging out in the now is you're always wet behind the ears, you know, fresh, innocent like a babe. No better way than that to catch a Zuvuya circuit without distorting it! But go back and tell them what you were gonna tell them, and I'll see if I can keep my Zuvuya-loving lips zippered!"

OK, Uncle Joe. Back to the meditation. Without this Zen part, our spirituality — I don't care what type it is — doesn't mean diddly-squat. Like Uncle Joe keeps saying, and I know he got it from John Lennon, "it's cleanup time." So let's get our electromagnetic brooms and hit those clogged-up, malfunctioning, life patterns and wave-forms. The planet is counting on us, you know! The planet is shouting out: "Hey humans! Come clean or you will be cleaned up!"

Now obviously we have problems here, each and every one of us. It's nice and artistic to describe the wave-forms, and how they mesh or don't mesh with each other, but how does this wave-form idea explain that each of us has problems and that the planet has a mega-problem: us? And how do we go about cleaning up our acts as efficiently as we can and yet at the same time be cleaning up the planet?

Here is how it has worked for me. I consider something I have done that frustrates me. And then I see that I have done it before, lots of times before. It seems like a dumb little thing, but what really bums me out about this is how many times I have done it. Why? Why does it repeat itself? Why does it become a pattern? Sometimes it is easy to isolate one of these patterns because it becomes an addiction, like drinking alcohol, smoking dope, or snorting cocaine. When you are doing those kinds of things every day, all the time, it is obvious: you have a problem.

There are a lot of problems that are less obvious, like the one in which we will always do the dishes, no matter what, and then secretly resent it — and others — for the situation. Or the one in which anytime someone gives us a compliment we will deny it, and then secretly torture ourselves, wondering if we really are beautiful or not, or what people really think of us.

OK. Now, from the point of view of the wave-forms, what is happening here is that we have run into *static*. In fact, your wave-form, my wave-form, and everybody's wave-form has ugly static clinging to it. And because the wave-form is electromagnetic, this clinging static short-circuits the Zuvuya memory hotline from delivering the goods that are truly needed for those situations in which we are frustrating ourselves. Bummer! Short circuit means just that: a teeny-weeny tape loop with a built-in memory reducer, so that it goes back and plays itself again . . . and again . . . and again. By reducing our memories, we reduce ourselves to limited, claustrophobic states of being.

The first step in cleaning up your wave-form is to know your personal wave-form. And to know your personal wave-form is to know the static that clings to it. This static is a negative vibration that is always attracting a negative situation of an equal frequency, and then leaving a trace of itself behind. These little electromagnetic traces or filaments that we leave behind are precisely why we have to clean up our act. They are ugly! If they don't catch up with us while we are alive, they will certainly be waiting for us when we die. As long as we deny that this is what is happening, it will continue to happen. We can rationalize these negative static-attractor situations any way we want. For example, "Oh, that's my past-life karma; nothing I can do about it." That is how it usually goes. Nonsense!

Now if we look at this negative, static, short circuit carefully, we will notice a few things. One, as a short circuit, it is hauntingly periodic. Two, it is a coverup. We are not facing something. We have all sorts of defenses around this static block. What is it covering up? What are we hiding?

What it is covering up is one of our imperfections. So we really can't drink, so what? In denying our allergy to alcohol, not only do we drink, but we invent all sorts of excuses and rationalizations for why we are doing it. And we actually come to believe all of the stuff we keep telling ourselves. Then we are really in trouble.

So we see that defense and denial are the allies of that ugly negative static which is clinging to our wave-forms. What we have to remember is that in denying our imperfections we are messing with our integrity. In messing with our integrity we are keeping our wave-forms from being attuned to themselves *and* to the planetary, solar, and galactic memory patterns. We are also closing ourselves off to our dimensional doubles, and keeping ourselves from becoming surfers of the Zuvuya. Look at all the benefits we are losing. Why do that? It's really a drag.

Remember, it is our imperfections that create our unique wave-forms. When we accept our imperfections we are in our wave-forms. Our wave-forms are functioning purely and cleanly. When our wave-forms are pure and clean, again and again they magnetize exactly what we need. Nothing more and nothing less. That is being in our integrity. And when we are in our integrity, then our wave-forms are radiant, as well as our bodies and auras. When our wave-forms are radiant they attract cosmic jollies. We are not going to run away from that, are we?

The key to remaining in our integrity is for each of us to *identify* with our own wave-form. This means to accept and love ourselves completely. Because we accept and love ourselves completely, we do not hide or deny our imperfections. Because we do not hide or deny our imperfections, we take complete responsibility for who and how we are. Because we take complete responsibility for who and how we are, we do not give our power away. By not giving our power away, we do not create negative cling static.

This negative cling static is like an electromagnetic block or negative attractor. The only reason it is located where it is located is because it corresponds to the place where we give away our power — those ugly electromagnetic traces or "astral loogies" as Uncle Joe calls them, that we leave in the wake of our disempowerment. The block is surrounded by bristling defense and denial mechanisms. This block is the emotional hook that keeps recreating the pattern of not loving ourselves. No joy in that!

The other side of the block is the projection of our own

powerlessness. This projection of our powerlessness, the negative attractor, can be our parents. It can be a drug. It can be an idea, an ideology, a religious belief, or the state of the world. Whatever it is, the projection of our powerlessness is not in or of our wave-forms. But it is the same exact shape as the static area in our wave-forms. It is like a blind spot, or a soft spot, that makes us defensive every time someone reminds us that it is there.

These disempowering blind spots are what make fundamentalists out of all of us. Fundamentalists choose to identify with and act upon the power given over to an outside authority rather than to stand in their own truth. When pushed, a fundamentalist will call upon the outside power to do everything it can to avoid the truth. In case you haven't gotten it, what we are talking about here are control issues. Control is the police action of disempowerment.

Taking back our power, standing in our own truth, accepting complete responsibility for ourselves and our actions, identifying with our own wave-forms — these acts are essential if we are going to participate in Earthlings Anonymous. And unless we participate in Earthlings Anonymous, we are going to have a heck of a time joining the Campaign for the Earth.

The Zen of the clean wave-form begins immediately once we admit that we have problems. When we honestly look and see what those problems are, then we say, "How are we going to do this? How are we going to get rid of the negative electromagnetic blocks, the clinging static that is making our wave-forms so unsightly?"

"Harmonic detergents, José," Uncle Joe zapped in again, "I told you it's harmonic detergents that you need to get rid of that ugly static cling and that waxy yellow build-up! Then you'll be singin', 'no static at all . . .'"

"Uncle Joe!" I called out in vain. Quicker than you can

bat an eyelash, Uncle Joe had come and gone. Fast wave he was riding. OK, back to Zen.

In the Zen of the clean wave-form, there are a few techniques that are like electromagnetic wave-form polishing cloths. First, there is sitting with our wave-forms, our total selves — habits, twitches, physical appearance, talents, energy levels, warts, the whole ball of wax. Second, there is self-love and complete self-acceptance. Third, there is self-empowerment, the act of taking back our power — all the energy we have been wasting on self-doubt and self-hatred.

The first polishing cloth, sitting with your wave-forms, is both the simplest and the hardest. You just sit. Nowhere to go, nothing to do. Keep your back straight and your eyes open. You can sit on a cushion on the floor, or you can sit on a chair, or you can sit outside on the Earth. The main thing is that you just sit and be present, with no preoccupations, in the silence — the great absorber. If you need to focus on anything, focus on your outbreath as it dissolves into space. There is nothing special about this. The point is to become familiar with your blocks, your short circuits.

To do this, I started with fifteen minutes to half an hour a day. For however long you can do it, you will notice certain very persistent themes. And you will notice your ego. I sure did, and so did Uncle Joe!

Your ego is the guy who won't let go. The ego's job is to maintain the static blocks. It is the controller. It is the secretary of defense. And it is the CIA mastermind of all denial mechanisms. So the point of sitting with your wave-form is also to become familiar with the ego. But it is tricky. It comes in lots of disguises which are also called ego trips, so it's good to learn them all. I'm still learning mine. But it's the sneaky, integrity-hating tricks which the ego uses that you really have to learn.

Sitting with our wave-forms, we can slowly begin to get

a handle on what things are keeping our wave-forms from
staying clean. If we can begin to get a handle on them,
then we can do something about them.

However if it was just a matter of watching, of sitting
in our wave-forms, we probably would not get very far.
We might just sit there bored with ourselves forever. That
is why it is so important to bring up the next polishing
cloth, the one that is called self-love and self-acceptance.

As you sit there watching your stuff, no doubt some of
it wants to make you puke. Sometimes you sit there thinking
over and over again, "I really am a low down, dirty, worth-
less sonuvabitch." Now what you have to keep in mind is
that that is exactly what your ego wants you to think. If it
can get you to think like that, then the ego has you in a
really nasty short circuit.

This is where the greatest antidote to static cling comes
into the picture: self-love and complete self-acceptance. If
we don't love and accept ourselves for exactly who we are,
nobody else will. This is the part where we forgive ourselves
for all of our imperfections. Maybe your fingers are too fat.
You are an alcoholic. You never got rid of the extra weight
you got when you had your third child. So what!

The thing we have to remember is this: imperfections
are like the flaws and inclusions in a crystal. It is those
flaws and inclusions that give the crystal its character. If we
leave our crystals in the sun, in time, some of those flaws
will turn into iridescent colored lights. That's the way it is
when we sit in our wave-forms and love and accept ourselves
completely. Our awareness and self-love are like the sun,
and the colors are the radiance of insight and memory
that come from knowing, loving, and accepting ourselves
completely.

Now comes the most radical move of all: taking back
our power. This, like the rest of it, is moment to moment.

We keep polishing all the time. But taking back our power happens in the heat of action. We know where our blocks are. We are in the middle of something and up comes a static block. With our awareness, we stand in the circle of our truth.

Our truth is the sum of our imperfections and how they give us our unique perspectives. Our perspectives define personal choice. The choice is to cover and hide, or to shine in our individual truths. The circle of truth is the boundary of each of our unique wave-forms. Polish on the spot. Leap. Take back our power! In a situation where we have been saying "no" all of our lives, we now say "yes!" Do it cleanly — no ugly trace filaments left behind. Now we are riding the wave, and the wind in our faces is the memory of our integrity returning to us in all of its innocence.

Doing all of this stuff, which is the nitty gritty of the Zen of the clean wave-form, is our responsibility. It is the individual way to restore our integrity. It is the most direct way to open our Zuvuya circuits, to set up clear dialogues with our dimensional doubles, and to begin to access those galactic and Atlantean memories. Above all, having clean wave-forms is to have happy galactic memory circuits. We don't want to miss out on that!

Now while it is our responsibility to keep those polishing cloths moving over our wave-forms, we cannot do this .whole thing alone. We need buddies. We need our sisters and brothers who are doing the same thing. That is where EA, Earthlings Anonymous, comes into the picture.

In EA, we admit before others our powerlessness over our static creating habits. We share our insights and revelations. We learn from others. And we affirm our intentions to maintain our integrity by identifying with our own wave-forms, by standing in our own truths, and by taking back our power.

It is a matter of cutting the *arrogance* that has come with being human and identifying all the time with disempowering human institutions. Instead, we assert that we are *Earthlings*. That is very important. "If you mudpies would cut all the uppity human crap and realize that you're Earthlings first," Uncle Joe says, "you sure could soar and fly, just like the birds circling in the channels of their own truths!"

When we identify with our wave-forms and understand that our wave-forms are *Earth* wave-forms, we put ourselves in tune with the Earth, and with the higher evolutionary intention of the Earth.

Participation in an Earthlings Anonymous group (you can call it whatever you want) is the first stage in the cleanup campaign, the Campaign for the Earth. Face it. If the Earth is going through purification, needing to get rid of its toxic wastes, and if we want to help, it won't do any good unless we are doing all we can to clean up our own acts, not leaving our own disempowered toxic wastes — those ugly static cling filaments — behind us.

As we get together with other "clean Earthlings," we get to the Crystal Earth Energy Network Home Improvement Association part of the process. This is the part where we begin to play triangles, to check out our resources, to hook up with other Home Improvement Association chapters, and to see what kind of moves are available for us to make.

Through the EA and the Home Improvement Association we get another bonus. We become On-Timers, or OTs. Any Mayan worth his or her salt is an OT, an On-Timer. Any clean wave-form which is the same as a Mayan, a surfer of the Zuvuya, is an OT. How is that?

When we are completely identified with our wave-forms, we are in synch — on-time — with ourselves. We have no short circuits, so we are also on-time with reality. Then, if we have a hook-up going with one or more other clean wave-forms, we have vertically tapped into the Big Circuit, the Zuvuya that takes us to Grand Central, Hunab Ku. Then we and our friends are on our way to becoming Grand Central OTs. That is hot. Our planet likes that. You can see why Zen is also a Mayan acronym: Zuvuya *Empowers Now!*

"You bet, José," Uncle Joe zinged in one more time, "OTs are always on the crest of the wave, the big now. You don't walk backwards on a wave. Just cruisin' with the synchronicity. That's smooth! That's radical! That's . . . stylin'!" With a splash of laughter he was gone, leaving a waft of sea spray and a mist of insight blowing about my wave-form.

Uncle Joe is right about this thing we call synchronicity. It is the tip of the big wave, the cosmic network, the interdimensional radio station. It is the splash of the galactic beam that invites us to become vertically hooked up and to surf our way to the evolutionary payoff by becoming . . . Warriors of the Zuvuya!

WARRIORS
OF THE ZUVUYA
OR BRINGING IT ALL
BACK HOME

"Warriors of the Zuvuya, surfing on the beam, catching a 25-year wave that'll hit evolutionary beachhead in 2012 AD. Clean Earthlings gathering their clans, forming their tribes, getting back to the garden, spending their time — doing what?" It was Uncle Joe. He was back inside my head again, mimicking me. "Fancy rhetoric boy, but how're you gonna deliver the goods?"

"Uncle Joe!" I called out, somewhat taken by surprise. "How have you been? It's felt kind of flat without you, but I've been doing OK. Tending my garden you know."

"I gathered that much. It felt pretty quiet from my end of things, too. Gave me time to pay attention to a few *special* upstairs kind of things."

"What *special* upstairs kinds of things do you mean, Uncle Joe?"

"See, at our last Higher Power Graduate Level AA meeting at the Midway Station, we had a visit from some of the Galactic Scouts, the Advance Guard, they call themselves. They represent the Arcturus Outpost 144. You know who's in that group? Pacal Votan!"

"No kidding, Uncle Joe! Pacal Votan?"

"You bet, Kid, Pacal Votan. I shouldn't tell you this, but ... Naw, better not."

"Tell me what, Uncle Joe?"

"Just that they mentioned your name. Something about ... watching your temper, not being so impatient."

I watched my emotions flip-flop as Uncle Joe spoke. But what did I expect? So far in this whole wild gambit the one thing I had noticed was that any sense of self-importance always gets knocked down. How could I make an exception of myself?

"You're fine with that, right Bud?"

"Sure Uncle Joe, after all I am a budding Earthling. How else do you learn? But tell me about the Arcturus Outpost 144 Galactic Scouts. What are they all about?"

"Of course, they've been monitoring things really closely. Minute details do not escape their attention. Naturally, the Maya have got a major stake in all of this. After all, they took on this planet as a major engineering project. They want to make sure it succeeds and that the project actually gets refunded in 2012 — Batkun 13 to them. For them it will be time for major colonization. Up till now they've only had an outpost here."

"Major colonization, Uncle Joe? That sounds ominous. I don't know if people here are going to go for that."

"The Scouts are aware of that. But it's not like it sounds or like you think it is. You see, being Mayan is being natural. It's living according to the cycles. When you're really in tune and living according to the cycles — the sun, the moon, the rotations of the planets, the tides — you're not hassled. You're actually riding the Zuvuya. It's going with the flow and at the same time, because you're really going with the flow, you're going beyond the flow. You go beyond the flow because being in tune with the universal cycle, you find the secret of all the cycles. And that's timelessness. Deathlessness. Now *that's* the big time!"

After a momentary pause, Uncle Joe started whistling, and then broke into a little song: "Up, down, all around, there is nothing to be found!"

"Neat little song, Uncle Joe," I replied, amused at his outburst.

"Remember, being a Mayan is being a master of illusion. See what I mean?"

"Sure do, Uncle Joe. So how does it look to them now? What is the post-Harmonic Convergence prognosis?"

"They're concerned. Very concerned. They're wondering if they got a bad deal from the evolutionary wholesaler. Bad genetic batch. You humans are giving them a case of interdimensional botulism. You can't cut the wars, the secret government drug stuff, or the economic manipulations to keep a gang of murderers holding the world in terror. Oppression, injustice, and corruption — that's what you've come to with your civilization and modern life! The whole thing's polluted — ego-chemical pollution! Civilization might be in the process of wiping out, but the aftereffects — you might say they can be felt from here to Kingdom Come! They're still wondering if they just shouldn't have a sudden death garage sale and scrap the whole lot of you."

"What? That sounds mean, Uncle Joe. I thought they were evolved upstairs."

"Sure they're evolved. But they've got things to work out, too. You know, that's one of the problems you've got in the third dimension. You think anything outside yourself is always going to be perfect. That comes from not accepting your own imperfections. And from living too one-dimensionally." Uncle Joe paused. After the last trip to the AA Midway Station, he seemed to be more wise than wise-guy.

"But that's the root of their concern," he continued in the

same reflective manner. "You humans got so bogged down in the the third dimension — that's your materialism — they don't know if you can all wake up from it. And even if you could wake up, they wonder if you've got the brains to clean up the mess you've made from living so one-dimensionally. On top of having to wake up and clean up, you also have to get with the evolutionary program. Remember, the object of this part of the evolutionary game is going interdimensional."

"No kidding, Uncle Joe. That's a tall order to fill in 25 years."

"Yep. Sure is. But you're on to something with this Warriors of the Zuvuya thing."

"Oh yeah, Uncle Joe?" I answered, happy at last to get a compliment of some sort. "What might that be?"

"Don't get too excited, now. I said you're *on* to something, I didn't say you had the answer. But listen, you're smart enough. You might get this."

"Don't tease me, Uncle Joe. We know we don't have much time now, so tell me what it is."

"OK. Your Warriors of the Zuvuya, I guess that's your term for your crack squad, the surfers who'll spearhead the Campaign for the Earth, well they sound like they're the ones the Galactic Scouts are looking for. You see, the Galactic Scouts, they've got their plan, too. They're lookin' for Earthlings willing to participate in Galactic Scouts Kindergarten."

Galactic Scouts Kindergarten! I loved it. In my mind I could see the sign for this Kindergarten hanging over the doorway that connected our planet to the galaxy and to other dimensions. Good. This was getting juicy now.

"And here's what it is, the plan: Return Engagement. They wanna come back. But it's gotta be colonized first."

"Colonized?" I said, realizing that we really hadn't dealt with this issue yet.

"Right, Bud. Like I said, the next phase of the Mayan Engineering team's job is to 'colonize' the planet. But that's not what you think it is. It's not a land grab or cultural genocide or any of the things you humans have been expecting us to do, yet have been doing for so long among yourselves.

"Look at it like this. Anytime a planet gets beyond the Atlantis stage — understands the right use of will, which is identifying with your own wave-form — well, anytime a planet gets past that final Atlantis, it goes Mayan. Yep, that's your Mayan Factor, Bud. That's how come they're so interested in what's happening here, Harmonic Convergence and all that. There's advanced Mayan civilization all over the galaxy. Wouldn't you want your planet to go Mayan, José? You know what that means, to go Mayan?"

As Uncle Joe asked his question, I could see pyramid temples and hear soft rhythms. But I knew there was more. "No, Uncle Joe, I don't know. Tell me what it means to 'go Mayan.' "

"Trying to keep it simple, Bud, it's like this. There's group energy and group mind. But no one's in there trying to steal your secrets — because you haven't got any secrets to steal! That secret stuff comes from fear. So there's no fear. If there's no fear, there's love. You're all channeling love. And you're still you with all of your uniqueness, only now you fit in. No more misfits. And there's no poverty, no war, no pain or disease, all that comes from thinking the wrong way about reality anyway. And what you're doin' everyday along with everyone else is hangin' out with the harmonics. Yeah, the ever-present, ever-lovin' harmonics. Your senses are all tuned and opened up and you're riffin' on the interdimensional fantastic!" Uncle Joe ended with a flourish on his kazoo.

"Going Mayan sounds great to me, Uncle Joe," I responded

enthusiastically. "But let's get back to this colonization thing."

"OK, Bud. So how it works is that you colonize yourselves first. You do that by letting your dimensional doubles
take over for you. Remember, these bodies you've got are
third-dimensional rentals. They're like space suits. It's us
dimensional doubles who are the *real* operators."

Now I was getting paranoid. Had Uncle Joe gotten
on a power trip? Would I be giving my personal power
away again?

"Relax, Bud." said Uncle Joe, reading my mind. "This is
the *big* challenge to your third-dimensional ego controls,
your petty ministers of defense. Hee hee hee! I mean, either
all that training you were laying down in the last chapter is
for real, or this evolutionary experiment is going to suck
it's own cosmic rotten eggs that it's been layin' and get
trashed something horrible."

"I get it Uncle Joe, just go on."

"Glad you and I have such meetings of the mind, José.
Makes my job easier, too. But back to the Return Engagement. Let's get this picture real clear now. Over the next
25 years, what's got to happen is that the humans have
to relinquish control and let their dimensional doubles
slowly assume the position of operators, like we're operating
machinery or something. Right now the machines are out of
control, trying to run themselves. Doesn't work that way.

"This is where your Warriors of the Zuvuya come into
the picture. They gotta take the lead. They've got to set an
example. You see what I mean?"

I swallowed hard. I saw all too well. "You mean, Uncle
Joe, just like you're my higher power and I'm handing
myself over to you?"

"You've been trained well! It's not bad either. At first it
seems scary and spooky, because you've believed for so long
that all there is is the flesh you can pinch. It's not like you'll

become a zombie. Sure, you'll become more and more like me. But do you dislike me? Am I bad? Have I really caused you any problems? Aren't I really like the zany child within you that still wants to hitchhike across the cosmos, listening to heavy metal, Arcturus-style, throbbing through your interdimensional fibers?"

Uncle Joe had me there. He nailed me to the truth of my own deepest desires. I really couldn't complain about him. What I could complain about were some of my own jerk-ass ego trips. But, so far, Uncle Joe was nothing but a straight shooter to me.

"OK José, you get the picture, like an instamatic camera with flash attachment! If you want to be a real Warrior of the Zuvuya, you'll just hand things over to me. Now. I won't make you sign a contract. But between you and me, we know that this is it. This is for real. You want to get on with the Campaign for the Earth, so therefore, by the power and authority invested in me I now *dub* you, Uncle Joe Zuvuya!"

"Holy shit! Now I'm Uncle Joe Zuvuya, too?"

"No big deal, José, you can call yourself whatever you want. But I know and you know who the real boss is. From here on out it's your dimensional double who is the operator calling the shots. You got interdimensional questions, just dial the operator — that's me. You've taken your first real step in surrendering control. Relax, man. Your wife will be tickled pink when she hears about this. After all, she's been on your case about this too, but you've been too proud to own up to it."

"Ok! Ok! OK!, Uncle Joe. A deal is a deal. We're on. After all, you're the one writing this book, not me. Truth's truth."

"Good show, m'boy. *In Lake'ch*, right, José? I am another yourself. Couldn't be more true. From here on out, we surf

together all the time. You're a bona fide Warrior of the
Zuvuya. You've got memory circuit rights. You've got galactic
databank access privileges. And, you've just entered Galactic
Scouts Kindergarten. Congratulations! You have now been
harmonically converged!"

"Harmonically converged! Wow! Thank you, Uncle Joe,"
I answered feeling emotional, my head swimming. I was
struggling to understand the implications of what had
just happened.

"Don't bother trying to understand; that's just more
control stuff," Uncle Joe interrupted my struggle with his
sage advice. "Let's get back to the Maya and their Return
Engagement. You've just experienced the first stage of the
kind of colonization which the Maya are anticipating will
pave the way for their return.

"As you surrender control and let your dimensional
doubles do the operating, you'll see that this one-dimensional
materialism thing is literally a drag, a gravity buster. And
another thing you'll see is that the cleanup thing can be
done as a form of interdimensional sport."

"Interdimensional sport? That's intriguing. What's that
all about, Uncle Joe?"

"Wait a sec, Surfer Pal. Before I get into that, there's
something I was supposed to tell you. Special message from
Pacal Votan.

"You know he does appreciate your efforts. But the
message wasn't anything personal. It was this: if you're
gonna be spreading around this Warrior of the Zuvuya
and Earthlings Anonymous stuff, you gotta mention that
it's *sacred*. That it's all sacred. You don't have to mention
God or anything religious. But you do have to mention
that all this activity is sacred and that the Earth and all
the universe is sacred, or else none of this would be
worth doing."

"That's cool, Uncle Joe. I'm with you."

"Yeah, José. That sacred business. You know what it really is?"

"Tell me, Uncle Joe."

"It's the stuff that breaks your heart, that makes you cry. That and nothing more. You can give it fancy names and that's fine too. But in the end, it's just the stuff that takes you by surprise and breaks your heart and leaves you crying for no good reason at all. And there's nothin' that can't do that to you, because it's all sacred."

"I think I get it, Uncle Joe." Inside I felt a release. Everything around me was shining in its own special light. I realized that life is so much stranger and more beautiful than we give it credit for.

"OK, José, snap out of it! Back to basics. You were asking me about this interdimensional sport."

"Oh, that's right. You were saying that the cleanup thing could be done as a form of interdimensional sport."

"See, once people start owning that they've got dimensional doubles and then let the dimensionals own them, then you've gotten to first base. That's already interdimensional sport. People'll be experiencing themselves and each other differently. People'll be having memories like they haven't had before. You had any of those kind of memories lately?"

"To tell you the truth, yes. I've been having memories of before I was born. And of other planets."

"Yeah, you've been around, Surfer Pal. Anyway, what's going to be happening is people will have to see this whole thing like a big play, a big show. Even like a big game. Like one of those game shows, only the object of this game will be this: to get around, take the whole thing down! Dismantle the factories of death. Let's have flowers growing in parking lots, freeways overgrown with grass. This whole industrial civilization gig has become a nightmare, anyway, a bad act that's come to its end, and it's time for a whole new show.

"The sooner you take the old industrial stage-set down, the faster you'll get around. It's like just as the lights are dimming on the one show, the lights begin to go on for the next one. That's your show. Now, you Warriors of the Zuvuya, you team players on the edge of the wave, will have to take some real risks and show 'em what you mean by getting around. This is especially important when the plug gets pulled . . ."

"When's the plug gonna be pulled?"

"Couple of years. It's all gonna be coming down. It's then that you really have to have your act together and show the people that what comes down is just going around. Big recycling time on planet Earth. Yeah, going down, coming round, bringing it all back home."

"Bringing it all back home, huh?" I responded. "Sounds too easy, Uncle Joe, and you were the one accusing me of fancy rhetoric. But listen, who's going to pull the plug?"

"You're right, José. It's not really gonna be easy. But it'll be a lot easier if you and all your friends get moving right now. Get your circles turning, get your Crystal Earth Energy Network Home Improvement Associations linked up, and be ready to go. Cuz when it shows that it's not going, when the value goes out of the money, and the Earth starts talking heavy weather, that's when the Home Improvement Associations gotta grab the spotlight on center stage.

. "If you're not on center stage when the plug is pulled, there's gonna be a lot of confused and angry people around. It's like when the ship tilts and starts to go down, you gotta be there with the lifeboats, boy."

Uncle Joe paused. A strange wind had picked up outside. Involuntarily, I shivered. Even though the sun was still shining, it was as if there were an eclipse. "And as for who's pulling the plug," Uncle Joe went on, "let's just say the plug is pulling itself. Or maybe it's not a plug, maybe it's like this big building that's been going up higher and higher — and as it gets higher and higher it also becomes wider and wider. At one point the base is too narrow, it's just one-dimensional, and crasho-whamo, down it all comes, like a house of cards unequal to the winds of change."

"I get the point, Uncle Joe."

"So when it comes down, you're going to be out there, Warriors of the Zuvuya, surfing up a storm, or I should say, surfing on the storm."

For a moment in my mind's eye, I saw the wave — dark and angry. It had already crested and was ready to come crashing down, boiling and furious.

"You see it clearly, Surfer Pal. That's Atlantis coming down. But this time it's not taking the world with it. If people aren't remembering Atlantis by 1989, they're sure gonna be remembering it by 1990.

"Let's not lose the light touch though. This is one of those moments when all you've got to go on is a song and a dance. And that's literally it. There's going to be a lot of healing to do, and you Zuvuya surfers are gonna be there with the goods. Center stage, yeah, with the Great Mayan Circle of Time Memory Show — 2012 or bust! Hee hee hee! You gotta show the people and make it real clear to 'em: yours is the best show in town. That way they'll be happy to join, 'cause this show allows *all* acts that lead to the interdimensional big-top!

"Now listen carefully," Uncle Joe shifted gears, like he was going to let me in on a big secret. "Upstairs, the Galactic Scouts mentioned something about a Planet Art Network being set up to match the Earth diving project. That's how this whole thing will begin to take on a new direction."

I was intrigued. Someplace inside of me, bells were ringing. "Now we're talking about something more positive,

Uncle Joe. Tell me more about this."

"OK. First of all, you Warriors of the Zuvuya, you've all gotta understand that you're artists. Nothing fancy, but artists of life, artists of reality, simply because you've got your wave-forms harmonized. Anything that's harmonized, that's art. Now, since anyone can potentially become a harmonized wave-form, or since everyone's wave-form is harmonic to start with, everyone's an artist. This is an important point.

"Another important point is that everyone who's identified with their wave-form, and who has 'em harmonized, well, they're also riding their Zuvuyas and teaming up with their dimensional doubles, right Uncle Joe?"

The rascal! Calling me Uncle Joe. "Wait a minute! You're calling *me* Uncle Joe, Uncle Joe?"

"Simmer down boy, that's the game now. In Lake'ch — I am another yourself."

"You're right, Surfer Pal," I answered him, mellowing into my expanded being.

Then Uncle Joe continued, "So, the point is that anyone who's got their wave-form harmonized is both an artist *and* an interdimensional player. Remember, don't be deceived by appearances, but become a master of illusion. And this isn't anything special. It's the way everyone can be, and, according to the evolutionary script, it's the way everybody should be. See where I'm going with this?"

"Sure do, Pal. It's like the Home Improvement Association has to have a kind of WPA, a Works Projects Administration, like in the Depression, only this time it's worldwide and it's called the Planet Art Network."

"Now we're cookin'!" Uncle Joe responded eagerly. "And since the planet's got to be cleaned up and re-harmonized, there isn't anything that isn't planet art. From taking down disgusting factories, to planting new forests. From remembering all the ways of barter, exchange, and give-away, to understanding how crystals channel the sun. From helping people get new images of life, to showing them how to become interdimensional. It's all retuning the body and senses for the greater harmony!

"And what's more, like I said, this has got to be done close to the Earth, in tune with the Earth diving project. Because you see, what those Earth divers will be doing is reactivating certain places on the surface of the Earth. This way the Earth will go interdimensional as well. In fact, Earth is ready to go interdimensional. We can help her. Once Earth is interdimensional — third and fourth dimensions at the same time — that'll be something! Spectral colors everywhere! Then the rest of us will go interdimensional a lot easier. And if we all want to go interdimensional together, there'll be a lot more doings close to those places that are being reactivated."

"I see, Uncle Joe. When you talk about those places being 'reactivated,' it will be like Harmonic Convergence, when people went to places like Stonehenge and Machu Picchu and Serpent Mound. That was like a sneak preview, huh?"

"You bet, Surfer Pal." Uncle Joe paused. I could feel his energy swirling around the top of my head, dropping down a little lower inside of me. "Reactivated also means that we're in touch with the energy of the Earth, of the sky, of the sun and moon and all the stars all at once. It's that sacred business again. Sacred is real. Sacred is the only real. That's the whole point. And remember, sacred is everything from your toenails and bleached hair to the cosmic swizzle stick that keeps the whole pot stirring!"

"Catch a wave, Uncle Joe, that's hot! But I have to know something. We know the Mayan engineering team has an investment in all this and that they are ready for a Return Engagement. But we have to do our work first. Tell me honestly. Do they think we have any chance at all of pulling this off, this Campaign for the Earth?"

"Yeah, they do. But you've got to go about it the right way. So far, what you've laid out is on the beam. But it's got to be done with the right attitude — balance play with sacredness, that's the way to do it.

"Watch out for anyone who says their scene is central headquarters, because in this project the only central headquarters is the Earth. And the Earth's central headquarters, well, it's down there in the crystal core where we went travelling, José. One other thing. The Galactic Scouts mentioned something about the Earth being the Grail, you know, like the quest for the Grail. King Arthur's court and all that.

"So you have to go about this like it's a sacred task. It *is* a sacred task. You become sacred warriors. Do it for the children, and it'll always remain sacred.

"That doesn't mean you don't have fun. Heck! If you're totally in your own wave-form, that's nothing but fun. But it is a sacred task. Earth's the Grail. You can figure that out. It hooks into Zuvuya riding and reactivating all those memories, right José?"

I let the silence be the answer. I looked long and deep into my heart. I knew that whatever my heart was holding on to had to be released. I knew that in that release I would lose nothing, but gain everything. I felt on the brink of a great adventure. What I was holding on to was my name, and whatever ambition went with it. "Let it go," I whispered to myself. "Let it go and let it grow."

"Hey, Jo-say! Don't get maudlin! I've got to get back for another meeting. Is there anything else you need before I split?"

I suddenly realized that Uncle Joe was indeed my better half, my higher power. "Yeah, Operator, there are at least a few things I need to know."

"Like what?"

"Well, I think I've got the script down pretty well. But didn't you mention that the Galactic Scouts wanted to send down a few galactic ambassadors. When is that going to happen again?"

"According to the Mayan engineering team, that's supposed to happen about 1992-93. That's just to check out how the first phase of the Campaign for the Earth has come along. Nothing special. But you've gotta get the people ready for it. You gotta get the network hooked up so that one day everyone dials up and what do they hear? 'Hello Atlantis!' That's right, 'Hello Atlantis!' That'll blow their amnesia circuits right out of the water.

"On the other hand, if you've been riding your Zuvuya circuits the right way, it'll all come together. The galactic emissaries will be here, ready with some crystal solar credits so you can buzz on the wireless and be launched for the last 20 years. No one should be *too* surprised. Why'd you ask though? Are you insecure or something?"

Suddenly, there he was, Uncle Joe Zuvuya sitting right there in front of me, scarcely four inches tall. "Whoa!" I cried out. "I thought you said you were splitting?"

"I will in a minute. But I just wanted to get something across to you before I go back up. As your dimensional double, I've got to tell you that you've come a long way. I couldn't do half the travelling around that I do if it weren't for where you're at. But you're still worrying." Uncle Joe then screwed up his face and took a long hard look at me. "One last piece of advice, José. Stop worrying!" Uncle Joe was looking mighty fierce now. Then he shouted at me in a way I had never heard him shout before. "Don't worry about a goddamned thing! Kick that last addiction out the other side of your wobbly wave-form!"

I felt pierced to the core of my being, right down to the root of my Kuxan Suum. Uncle Joe was still staring at me, penetrating me with his interdimensional gaze.

"You see, José," his voice was soft again, almost like a whisper. "Whatever you worry about, it doesn't matter. It still affects the planet's atmosphere, which is very sensitive. And the planet's atmosphere doesn't need any more worry. So cut out your worrying — now!

"Just follow your path, José. Follow your path and trust. Don't seek anything, and don't do anything because you think you'll get something out of it by doing it. Just do what you need to do. Everything is going to be all right. We're all standing in the planet's field of intelligence, every single one of us. You gotta be ready for its changes, its little adjustments. If you're worrying when the planetary field of intelligence changes, then you miss it. You miss the moment for memory access and retrieval. And that could be the *critical* moment!

"Don't get any illusions, José. You've still got a long way to go. But worrying isn't gonna get you there any faster. And if you do fall out of your integrity, especially then, don't worry! Being out of integrity is just a sign to get you back into it! So don't lose heart, that's the bottom line. You and all your Surfer Pals have got everything you need for the ride.

"And remember this. Your Zuvuya circuit goes back — and forward — longer than you. Take a lot of time to be quiet so you can access those memories.

"And the Maya have been around just as long as your Zuvuya circuit. They're patient. Their mindfield is vast. They're the children of the Sun. They knew Atlantis, not only here but on many other planets in many other star systems. The Maya have left clues in many places, including the planet you call Mars. Wherever harmony is the first

order of the day, the Maya are nearby, watchful and caring.
Harmony is their sign. The natural harmony of mind with
nature is their path and their goal. Just tuning into that
harmony tunes you into the Mayan wavelength. Every day
that arises is a Mayan melody, a solar chord knocked out
in a new galactic key.

"Harmonic Convergence wasn't just another galactic
Mayan holiday. It was an awakening in the heart of the
people to the common Zuvuya circuit that leads through
the Earth to the stars. The central computer in the Earth's
crystal core is gearing up for the next master program from
Grand Central, Hunab Ku. Don't doubt any of this, José.
Just get the word out. And don't fall for people's needs for
a messiah or a hero. That's a setup to make you a hit-man
in the wrong shooting gallery. In this show, everyone's got
to be their own hero or heroine. Get the Crystal Earth Energy
Network Home Improvement Associations to link up their
own computer network and have it link up with Earth's
central computer and nothing's going to stop you."

Before I could say, "Wow, Uncle Joe, that's eloquent!"
he was gone. All that was left was the afterimage of his
plume of iridescent hair fluttering a few inches above me. I
could feel the interdimensional wisp of him breezing toward
the Arcturus-Antares Midway Station, his favorite haunt,
for another 12-step meeting.

On the table nearby was one of my favorite Earth
medicines, a small, amethyst crystal wand. I looked long
and hard at its deep interior spaces, its swirling cloud
databanks of timeless information, its flashing flames of
iridescent light. It, too, spoke to me.

"Oh brother, I am as near to you as the stars. I am the
voice of the Earth. I am your heart's speaking stick. I am
the mirror of your confidence. Do not depart from your
wave-form. Speak always from the circle of your truth.

Experience is your only guide. Do not doubt it. This story you have told is no idle fabrication. Always be kind to yourself, and keep the thought of others' welfare before you as a star that draws you ever on."

These words echoing in my heart, I got up and walked to the door. Time to go out. Time for a breath of air. There, beneath the vast canopy of stars in the predawn chill, I knew it was time . . . to return to the Earth.

2 LAMAT 14 MAC APRIL 6, 1988
The Northern Year 8 IX
Year of the Sorcerers
of Harmony

EPILOG

Merlyn
A Song of The Crystal Earth

Merlyn
Nightseer
Who writes the crystal script
whose spectral robe
is the spiralling filament staircase
down which the 13 galactic rays descend
into Camelot's subterranean lake
where untold fragments of the one dream
swirl in luminous self-absorption
emitting strange electrical charges
attracting to each other
their own forgotten sources

Merlyn
surrendering to you
following you
I arrive at last
at the deepest point of your realm
the innermost Earth
which is also
the flight room
of the mighty crystal ship
Excalibur

And there
in the Temple
called Refuge of the Dragon and the Grail
Merlyn's apprentices
Andor, the dragon-witted warrior
and Vi-El, the Grail-weaving far starborn princess
Stir the cauldron of unconditional love
no common mix
and yet this brew
pulsing with the harmony
of all the stars we have ever called home
bubbles and seeps through
the portholes connecting the larger collective soul-body
of this dear Earth
to its myriad individual dream bodies
ourselves
now caught in our postures
of aggression, conflict and confusion

"Stir! Stir! Stir!"
Merlyn cries
"Make sure the recipe is correct
Mix in it the formulae
that will register in the dreamers
as the alchemy of love
and the desire for magic
as ceremonial
as the sun is pure!
Stir! Stir! Stir!"

This Earth is aching breaking shaking
its dream dragon body restless to emerge
crouches at the edge of the known
waiting for that ripe moment
to appear in all its rainbow wonder

O you apprentices of the crystal flight room
of Excalibur
Refuge of the Dragon and the Grail,
Andor and Vi-El,
I call to you from my sleep
on behalf of all the dreamers
of this planet
stir the potion well
that the Grail may appear
from within the dragon's
coiled tail
its cloud banks bursting
with light never before seen
by eyes of flesh

O Merlyn
from the rocks of Earth's far-flung island realms
appear simultaneously
in all of your shape-shifting forms
speaking the dawn
writing the power of the dream
with your crystal script
now
I call upon you
now
to cast your pan-harmonic spell
to wake the dreamers all
and stop their march
through this living hell
O Andor and Vi-El
cook in glee
the potion that returns
all memory
for now I must awake with all

into the greater dream
or not awake at all

received 3 Cib 2 Mac, March 25, 1988
transcribed 6 Cauac 5 Mac, March 28, 1988
by the faithful servant of the Zuvuya
Uncle Joe

Prayer of the Seven Galactic Directions

From the East House of Light
May wisdom dawn in us
So we may see all things in clarity

From the North House of Night
May wisdom ripen in us
So we may know all from within

From the West House of Transformation
May wisdom be transformed into right action
So we may do what must be done

From the South House of the Eternal Sun
May right action reap the harvest
So we may enjoy the fruits of planetary being

From Above House of Heaven
Where star people and ancestors gather
May their blessings come to us now

From Below House of Earth
May the heartbeat of her crystal core
Bless us with harmonies to end all war

From the Center Galactic Source
Which is everywhere at once
May everything be known as the light of mutual love

OH YUM HUNAB K'U
EVAM MAYA E MA HO!

ACKNOWLEDGMENTS

Surfers of the Zuvuya is a book born of the turbulent waters of our time. To acknowledge those people and forces who contributed to its coming into being is to acknowledge the interdependence of all of life on this planet at this time, as well as those galactic forces currently interfacing with our planetary,existence. That's cosmic enough, but I mean it — and so does Uncle Joe!

But to be cosmic, Zuvuya-style, is to be next of kin. It is to those people closer to home, my kin and neighbors, the plain-speaking folk to whom this book most owes its existence. Originally, before my son Josh died, I was going to dedicate this book to my older sister, Laurita, and my twin brother, Ivan, for the love they have shown me through the years. My sister particularly needs acknowledging for the unique inspiration she provided me during and immediately after Harmonic Convergence. Because of her, I knew I wanted to write something that would speak to her.

Whether I succeeded or not in writing something closer to my sister's language, I do know that the voices of Josh's friends Dylan, Joe, Kell, Scotty, Surrey, Matt, and Blaine, among others — might be heard in the pages of this book, and I acknowledge all of their inspiration and support. Then there is Josh's sister, my daughter, Tara, a true warrior spirit whose example and whose friends are also laughing through the pages of this book. My stepchildren, Paul and Heidi, are also to be acknowledged for their wise knowing and brilliant ways.

A totally special place goes to my wife, Lloydine, harmonizer of energy through Jin Shin Jyutsu, whose loving support, intimacy, and willingness to always go the next step have kept me anything but straight! Lloydine's mother, Maya, also deserves mention for her unquenchable enthusiasm for my work and her readiness to read early draft versions of *Surfers of the Zuvuya*.

Then there are those close to me, my neighbors and friends who showed so much support and loving kindness during the difficult time accompanying the writing of this book. These include that ace geomant and New Age coyote, Gary Raper, as wise as one could wish a friend to be; Laura Olsen, whose birthday is the same as my sister's and whose kindness always appears without asking for it; Harry and Lyn Loy, beautiful and daring surfers cruising at the far edge of the expected, along with their fantastic surfer twins, Sara and Jenna; and Russ and Lyn McDougal, artists of life drinking the wine of untold mirth.

Other voices and talents to be acknowledged are those of my Santa Fe friends, most notably Dee Treadwell, whose cranium has been tapped by the galactic memory reconstruction crews, much to his and my benefit, and his sensitive and powerful teammate, Linda Childers. And to Jamie Sams, that wild Texan Druid wolf priestess, special mention goes for her exquisite editing of *Surfers* — and for her cosmic cooking on all levels and burners.

Also in Santa Fe is the publishing clan known as Bear & Co. In Gerry Clow, the publisher, I am discovering not only a sensitive businessman, but a brother Aquarian visionary — our path and our journey have scarcely begun. To Barbara Clow, yet another Aquarian visionary, I owe a deep gratitude for her editorial skills, her deeply intuitive insights, and abiding support. Gail Vivino is acknowledged for the clarity of her final editing instructions, which helped bring out the full artistic integrity of the book. Finally, I wish to acknowledge the friendliness, caring, and creativity of the staff of Bear & Co.; their kindness and readiness to serve is exemplary.

ABOUT
THE AUTHOR

Artist, poet, visionary historian, and cosmic harmonist, Dr. Argüelles is recognized as a leading spokesperson for the principles of art as awakened warriorship and the role of art as a dynamic agent of planetary transformation. His master-piece of synchronistic analysis, *The Mayan Factor: Path Beyond Technology*, unraveled the prophetic harmonic code of the ancient Mayan civilization and initiated the Earthwide Harmonic Convergence consciousness-shift celebrations of August, 1987.

Argüelles was the founder of the First Whole Earth Festival. As a transformational art activist, he went on to found the Planet Art Network in 1983 as a visionary instrument for global artistic change. Since 1983, Argüelles and his wife, Lloydine, have travelled extensively promoting "Art as a Foundation for Global Peace."

Argüelles holds a Ph.D. in art history from the University of Chicago. As an educator, university professor, poet, art critic, and philosopher, his work has appeared in many journals of art, philosophy, and leading-edge thought. His books include: *Mandala* (coauthored with Miriam T. Argüelles); *The Transformative Vision: Reflections on the Nature and History of Human Expression; The Mayan Factor: Path Beyond Technology;* and *Earth Ascending: An Illustrated Treatise on the Law Governing Whole Systems.* Dr. Argüelles is currently program coordinator of creative arts at the Union Graduate School in Cincinnati.

BOOKS OF RELATED INTEREST
BY BEAR & COMPANY

EARTH ASCENDING
An Illustrated Treatise on the Law Governing Whole Systems
by José Argüelles

ECSTASY IS A NEW FREQUENCY
Teachings of The Light Institute
by Chris Griscom

THE MAYAN FACTOR
Path Beyond Technology
by José Argüelles

MEDICINE CARDS
The Discovery of Power Through the Ways of Animals
by Jamie Sams & David Carson

MIDNIGHT SONG
Quest for the Vanished Ones
by Jamie Sams

THE UNIVERSE IS A GREEN DRAGON
A Cosmic Creation Story
by Brian Swimme

Contact your local bookseller or write:
Bear & Company
P.O. Drawer 2860
Santa Fe, NM 87504